THE 1-2-3 MONEY PLAN

The Three Most Important Steps to Saving and Spending Smart

Gregory Karp

Vice President, Publisher: Tim Moore
Associate Publisher and Director of Marketing: Amy Neidlinger
Executive Editor: Jim Boyd
Editorial Assistant: Myesha Graham, Pamela Boland
Operations Manager: Gina Kanouse
Digital Marketing Manager: Julie Phifer
Publicity Manager: Laura Czaja
Assistant Marketing Manager: Megan Colvin
Cover Designer: Alan Clements
Managing Editor: Kristy Hart
Project Editor: Betsy Harris
Copy Editor: Karen Annett
Proofreader: Debbie Williams
Indexer: Lisa Stumpf
Senior Compositor: Gloria Schurick
Manufacturing Buyer: Dan Uhrig

Pearson Education LTD.
Pearson Education Australia PTY, Limited.
Pearson Education Singapore, Pte. Ltd.
Pearson Education North Asia, Ltd.
Pearson Education Canada, Ltd.
Pearson Educación de Mexico, S.A. de C.V.
Pearson Education—Japan
Pearson Education Malaysia, Pte. Ltd.

Library of Congress Cataloging-in-Publication Data

Karp, Gregory.
   The 1-2-3 money plan : the three most important steps to saving and spending smart / Gregory Karp.
      p. cm.
   ISBN 0-13-714173-4 (pbk. : alk. paper) 1. Home economics—Accounting. 2. Consumer education. 3. Budgets, Personal. 4. Finance, Personal. I. Title. II. Title: One two three money plan.
   TX326.K27 2009
   332.024—dc22
                                                        2008054616

For Rebecca, Jacob, and Michael

Contents

Acknowledgments

Wisdom in this book does not come from me alone.

The great information herein can be largely attributed to the many experts who have agreed to talk with me through the years.

Wisdom also comes from readers of my national newspaper column, "Spending Smart," and my previous book, *Living Rich by Spending Smart*. Literally hundreds of readers have called and e-mailed to ask questions, share their collective wisdom and experiences, or just thank me for providing straightforward advice, which is the only way I know how to give it. They are a continuing inspiration to tackle new spending topics each week in my column and pursue larger publishing projects. For all of those collaborators, I am grateful.

I'd also like to thank editors at the *Morning Call* newspaper in Allentown, Pennsylvania, where I work. Editor Ardith Hilliard and managing editor David Erdman have been supportive of my national newspaper column, "Spending Smart," which is published in Tribune Company newspapers. They have also made allowances for my nonnewspaper writing.

Thanks to Jim Boyd, executive editor at FT Press, and reviewers Russ Hall and Michael Thomsett. A special thanks to Jeanne Bonner for meticulously reviewing the manuscript.

Thanks, too, to Clark Howard, author and host of the *Clark Howard Show* on radio. Clark's encyclopedic knowledge of consumer issues is an inspiration. One conversation with him, in particular, led to the idea for the format of this book—of providing just three tasks for each money topic.

To family, friends, and colleagues who have taken an interest in my books, thank you. Your support means a lot.

Most important, thanks to my immediate family—Rebecca, Jacob, and Michael—for your support and accommodation as I finished two books in 15 months. Your love and understanding mean more than you know.

About the Author

Gregory Karp is an author and journalist of 20 years. His national newspaper column, "Spending Smart," is published in papers that together have millions of readers. The weekly column appears in the *Chicago Tribune, Baltimore Sun, Hartford Courant, Orlando Sentinel, Allentown Morning Call,* and others. The column has three times won a Best Column Award from the Society of American Business Editors and Writers.

He is also author of *Living Rich by Spending Smart: How to Get More of What You Really Want.*

Greg's advice on spending money smarter has appeared in national magazines, such as *Newsweek* and *SmartMoney;* television broadcasts, such as WCBS in New York, WSB in Atlanta, and WPVI in Philadelphia, and literally dozens of newspapers nationwide, from the *Los Angeles Times* to *Newsday* in New York.

He maintains a Web site at www.gregkarp.com and blog at SpendingSmart.net.

Greg lives near Philadelphia with his wife and two sons.

Telling It Straight

This book is, admittedly, a low-tech device. But it's meant to offer advantages you find in a high-tech GPS navigation system for your vehicle and an iPod audio player.

In navigating money and spending issues, especially in these challenging economic times, I hope you'll find this book as helpful and succinct as a GPS device that gives driving directions in an unfamiliar region. And in simplicity, it's meant to be as easy to use as the ubiquitous iPod music player.

Fortunately, you don't have to be a gadget lover to use it.

Getting from Here to There

I like my GPS navigation system, a Garmin Nuvi. I suggest you buy one, after you get your money life in order and are spending your money smarter every day.

No. It doesn't have to be that brand or model of GPS navigator. There are many good ones—ones with different features and less-expensive ones that still get the job done. But, the Garmin Nuvi is a very good line of GPS systems for nearly everybody. And if you drive often in unfamiliar areas, you should buy one.

This brief suggestion is indicative of this book. I intend to give you very specific advice about spending and handling money.

"Garmin," as I unimaginatively named my GPS system, tells me, turn by turn, how to get from where I am now to where I want to go. I don't mean that it lists directions and a map on a screen. While I'm driving, a voice inside the small box mounted on my dashboard speaks directions and road names—albeit, sometimes with butchered pronunciations.

Garmin doesn't care where I started, even if I'm lost to begin with. And it doesn't always give me the absolute-best route to where I'm going. But Garmin gets me where I'm going, almost every time.

Garmin also provides me peace of mind. While driving in unfamiliar areas with confusing traffic patterns, I don't care that Garmin isn't providing the absolute-best directions—directions that might get me to my destination two minutes sooner. I care that it gives me clear, understandable directions and gets me where I'm going safely.

In an unfortunate parallel world, Garmin might have a fatal flaw. It might have a Shakespearean Hamlet complex, contemplating "To be or not to be." It would be much less useful.

What if at every intersection it spoke something like, "Turn left on Maple Street...or go two blocks and turn left on Main Street...or, if you're in a hurry, avoid the upcoming busy intersection and cut through the Cherry Blossom housing development on the left...or if this is rush hour, make a U-turn and take the on-ramp to the bypass"?

Huh? Driving at 40 miles per hour and with little time to make a decision, directions that offer every route would be nearly useless. How am I to choose the best route of those given? "Garmin, that's what I paid *you* to do!"

And so it is with financial advice.

Consumers view many financial books as they would the indecisive GPS navigator. The books typically provide a confusing array of money advice that covers every possible situation. Advice is rendered nearly useless because the consumer has to make several complicated decisions he or she feels ill-equipped to make. The reader ends up needing advice in order to take the advice.

Sometimes, you just need a Garmin to tell you what to do. This book intends to be your Garmin in navigating money issues, so you can get where you want to go, with as little confusion as possible.

If I may stretch the metaphor one last time: When I'm driving and I disobey Garmin—refusing to "turn left" or "take the ramp on the right" as instructed—Garmin simply recalculates new directions for me based on where I am now. You see, though Garmin is giving me specific advice, I retain the right to choose my own way.

And so it is with this book. University of Chicago professor Richard Thaler, the father of the study of behavioral economics, calls it *libertarian paternalism*. Basically, it means that leaders can use what we know about consumer behavior to get people to do the right things for themselves. So, in this book, I will nudge you in a direction that is likely to be good for you. That's the paternal part. But, of course, you retain the free will to modify or disregard the advice and choose a different direction. That's the libertarian part.

This book does not restrict your freedom to choose. Nor does it advocate blindly following advice without understanding it. You have the power to customize the advice to your own life. The benefit of the book is providing you with a framework for making decisions, and at the very least, showing you what a good decision looks like.

Simple as an iPod

If you want to discuss simplicity, it's hard not to talk about Apple's iPod digital music player. This handheld device allows you to move music, audiobooks, and even movies and TV shows from your computer to the device for on-the-go listening and viewing.

Arguably, it is not the absolute-best music player on the market. Others offer more features and even better audio quality, some reviewers claim. Many are less expensive. But none is easier to use. And for that reason, the iPod blows away the competition in sales. And for that reason, I recommend you buy an iPod if you're interested in taking your audio and video with you.

My in-laws wanted a digital music player. Knowing I'm a gadget guy, they asked me what I would recommend.

In my mind, answering this question is complicated calculus. That's because I'm aware of the many offerings among music players. I know the iPod's strengths and shortcomings. I could have given them a dissertation on all the available models of music players and all the possible features they could get. After hearing all that, my in-laws' minds would surely be swimming with a slew of seemingly disconnected facts and considerations. They would have to make a long series of complicated prerequisite decisions just to make the one decision they cared about: buying a music player.

In answering their question, the lengthy dissertation played inside my head, but what I said was this: "Get an iPod. It's the easiest to use. You'll love it."

And they do.

Easy Is Hard

This might be at once the most controversial and most helpful money book you have ever read.

Why?

Because I'm going to give you very specific advice on what to do to handle your money better and improve your spending habits. I'm going to name names and tell it straight.

For example, I'll tell you to invest in index mutual funds. If you're having trouble choosing a company to buy index funds from, go with Vanguard. You won't be disappointed. I'll tell you never to buy an extended warranty—ever. I'll suggest what type of wireless cell phone plan to get—or switch to. Where it's impractical to give specific brand names—maybe because offerings change too quickly—I'll tell you specifically, step-by-step, how to determine for yourself how to choose.

The wonderful secret of personal finance nowadays is much of it is "set it and forget it." There are things you have to do once and never bother with again until your life circumstances change. You can put your bills on autopilot and set up an investing plan and not worry about it.

Taking decisive stands in advice-giving is risky, especially for a journalist like me who is accustomed to providing both sides of the story. And I'll concede up front that people's financial situations do, in fact, differ. But so many people are overwhelmed with the numerous choices for spending and investing their money that they freeze. It's too easy to get the deer-in-the-headlights look and do nothing at all. In that way, the massive financial tomes that attempt to cover every option actually do a disservice.

This is borne out time and again, as I read through and respond to hundreds of e-mails every year from readers of my "Spending Smart" newspaper columns published in Tribune Company newspapers. These readers don't want to know what all the options are, necessarily. They want quality advice on what they should *do*. What specific action should they take?

An acronym we learned as children is appropriate when dealing with money. It is KISS. It stands for *Keep It Simple, Stupid*. With money, simple does not mean unsophisticated. You can keep it simple and KISS your money worries good-bye.

Ask any financial adviser about it: Some people just want to be told what to do. They will not invest the time and effort to learn about a subject and investigate all the alternatives. They're sitting ducks for rip-offs, bad spending decisions, and, at best, money mediocrity.

This book will infuriate some people, those whose livelihoods depend on making finances as confusing as possible in the areas of investing, insurance, and telecommunications, for example. It will infuriate some companies whose products are not recommended in favor of their competitors' offerings.

However, it will help the average consumer take control of his or her money life with minimal effort, allowing the person to make better spending decisions every day.

When Good Enough Is Good Enough

I don't pretend to proffer only original ideas. After all, details change but the basics of personal finance remain the same throughout time. Writings from the Bible to Benjamin Franklin visit the same themes about money.

My contribution is taking literally volumes of information and boiling them down to what you need to know. Granted, it's what *I think* you need to know. And what I think is based on what's safe and what's "good enough."

I heard the concept of good enough expressed most clearly when I was interviewing personal finance guru Jean Chatzky about her book, *Make Money, Not Excuses*. She didn't invent the concept of good enough, but that's where I heard it, so I'm more than happy to give credit.

"The truly great thing about 'good enough'—and the reason it is so powerful—is that it allows you to get to the starting line in a way that waiting for the ultimate, best possible result does not," Chatzky writes.

Good enough means just that. Every money decision doesn't have to be the very, absolute best you could possibly do. Sometimes good enough is good enough. You will accomplish your goals. Get it done and get on with your life. After all, so many of us don't want to devote innumerable hours to dealing with our finances and picking nits with our spending.

"Give me something appropriate and smart to do, and I'll be happy with that," some people think.

Of course, other people are wired to always want the best, to strive for ultimate excellence in all they do. This works well in some areas of life, but not so well with money.

To those people, I would contend that sometimes good enough is, in fact, well above average. Go back to the topic of index mutual funds. With index funds, you'll get decidedly average returns—essentially whatever a market index returns. Yet most people would do far better if they invested in simple, boring index funds, rather than pursuing elusive market-beating returns. Instead of juggling a retirement portfolio of wide-ranging and overlapping investments, most would be best served in a low-cost target-date fund composed of index funds. It's simple, and you're virtually guaranteed to do better than most investors because index funds outperform two-thirds to three-quarters of actively managed (stock-picking) funds. Index funds and target-date funds more than qualify as "good enough."

We need to do smart things with our money, but we'll drive ourselves crazy wading through thousands of options in a hopeless quest for that absolute-best thing. Sometimes good enough is good enough.

Is This Book Different from Living Rich by Spending Smart?

My previous book, *Living Rich by Spending Smart: How to Get More of What You Really Want*, covered a lot of ground. It provided literally hundreds of tips about spending. Feedback from readers was overwhelmingly positive. Even true cheapskates seemed thrilled to find tips they had never seen before.

I was struck by one poignant comment left by a reader on the book's Amazon.com Web page:

"I'm age 70. *Living Rich [by] Spending Smart* has opened my eyes as to how much money I have thrown away. I hate this book. It makes me ashamed of myself. On the other hand, this knowledge will make living entirely on Social Security a lot easier."

Of course, the book's goal was to inspire smarter spending rather than induce shame. But the point is that many people found it changed the way they think about spending.

This book is different. Though it touches on some of the same topics, it is altogether unlike the first one. This book provides concrete structure and linear sequence to the many money issues that too often seem to move like wafting puffs of smoke in a breeze.

Instead of striving to deliver more tips, we endeavor to visit fewer—only the important ones most likely to be useful to you.

A bigger difference, however, is this book pushes ahead, beyond spending. We talk about many aspects of your financial life, such as improving your credit rating, planning for retirement, and paying for kids' college expenses. Of course, we look at those areas with an eye toward spending and saving smarter.

How to Use This Book

You, no doubt, already accomplished some of the money tasks outlined in this book—maybe many of them. However, I'm sure you'll excuse me if I start each topic from ground zero, assuming you've done nothing. For example, I'll tell you to get a will, so when you die your survivors will have direction. If you already have a will, check it off the list and move along. But being reminded isn't a bad thing. It might just jog your memory to complete that money task you've been meaning to get to. It might list a useful Web site you've never visited. It might provide a philosophy that changes your thinking about saving and spending money.

The Power of Three

This book uses the rule of threes by providing three main tips for each subject. For some reason, human brains do well with information that comes in packets of three. It seems to be the ideal number. Think about it:

- Life, liberty, and the pursuit of happiness
- Location, location, location
- Sex, lies, and videotape

There are often three characters in a story: the three stooges, the three little pigs, and the three musketeers. Survivalists claim humans can live for three weeks without food, three days without water, and three minutes without air.

The rule of threes has been a comedian's tool forever. It's why jokes start: "Three guys walk into a bar" and "A priest, a rabbi, and a minister."

- "How do you get to my place? Go down to the corner, turn left, and get lost."
- "I know three French words: Bonjour, merci, and surrender."
- "I can't think of anything worse after a night of drinking than waking up next to someone and not being able to remember their name, or how you met, or why they're dead." *Laura Kightlinger, entertainer*

So, topics in this book endeavor to keep your to-do lists to three tasks, keeping it as simple as 1-2-3.

This book doesn't address every last money issue in your life, but it does give you tools and ideas to save and spend money smarter. You don't need to implement all of the advice immediately, but you do need to get started today.

Chapter 1

Spending Smart Redux

What Is Spending Smart?

Before we proceed, I should define one phrase, so we are on the same page—both figuratively and literally, as it turns out. The phrase is *spending smart*.

Spending smart is a specific philosophy for achieving financial security without depriving yourself. It is not a cheapskate plan. It's about spending your money smarter on things you're buying every day anyway. It abides by the notion that you can't outearn dumb spending. Just ask all the millionaire celebrities, professional athletes, and lottery winners who end up broke.

Let me repeat for emphasis: You can't outearn dumb spending.

Spending smart aims to plug the leaks of wasteful spending and redirect money to things you truly care about.

Spending smart can pervade every aspect of your money life. It is so powerful that it can mean the difference between struggling and living rich.

Spending smart is important now more than ever. With the meltdown of banking and financial systems in the fall of 2008, credit became more difficult to get, the stock and bond markets tanked, and consumers clamped down on spending. All of a sudden, frugality was not only hip and cool, but necessary.

And we have more marketing coming at us than ever before—on the television, newspapers, magazines, radio, Internet, and billboards, to name a few. This bombardment of messages enticing us to buy stuff means we have to say no. If we didn't say no, we'd go broke in no time flat. We have to say no literally dozens of times a day. We have to say no so often that we can become weak, weary, and vulnerable as consumers.

We also have available credit like never before. There was a time when no money meant no buying. Not today. These days, you can charge it today and pay for it whenever. Saying no becomes that much harder when we have enough credit to buy.

Spending smart is about making good decisions when saying yes. It's not always about spending less, but squeezing more value from the money you're already spending. It's not about deprivation. It's about liberation.

So, before we dive into very specific advice in the next chapter, let's briefly look at what this notion of spending is all about.

When to Spend Your Money

Money is only good for one thing—spending it. The question is *when* you spend it. So, that's how we'll break down topics in this book. The following provides a brief overview.

When to Spend Your Money, 1-2-3

1. **Today.** Spend smarter on current expenses.
2. **Yesterday.** Pay debt.
3. **Tomorrow.** Save money for spending later.

1. Spend Today

Spending today encompasses your current expenses. It's so important because you make dozens of spending decisions every day. You decide whether to buy or not to buy, whether to purchase item A or item B. And you decide to buy now or buy later. The sum result of all these daily decisions determines whether you struggle or prosper with money.

The secret to successful money management has not changed throughout time: You must spend less on current expenses than you earn. How do you do that without depriving yourself? You spend your money smarter, every day.

2. Spend Yesterday

Spending yesterday is a way of saying that you should finish paying for stuff you bought in the past. In other words, pay off debt. This is a powerful type of spending and should be a priority, especially for consumer debt, such as credit cards and auto loans.

Debt, used irresponsibly, can be insidious. Its destruction goes far beyond dollars and cents. For many people, debt creates a level of stress that makes the original purchase entirely regrettable.

3. Spend Tomorrow

Spending tomorrow refers to saving and investing. Many people seem to think that saving is different from spending. Really, it's just deciding to spend at some point in the future, such as when your child goes to college or when you retire. Of course, this goes against our very nature. As humans, we're hardwired to consume immediately. It's instinctual. It's how we evolved. So, saving takes a lot of intellect and discipline. It requires us to fight back against our inner caveman (or cavewoman).

That's why successful savers make it automatic. They stop fighting their instincts and live in blissful ignorance. For example, most people find automatic paycheck deductions that go into their 401(k) retirement plans quite painless. They don't miss the money going to savings. But sitting down every month and writing a check to deposit into your IRA? That takes a whole different level of discipline, especially over long periods of time.

Regular saving and investing is important because most people working regular jobs don't have enough hours in the day to build wealth from a wage or salary. You have to force your money to make its own money, whether through compound interest, stock-market gains, investing in your own profitable business, whatever. It's the only way people of average means will build wealth.

Of course, these three concepts are intertwined. If you can't get a handle on daily spending, you can't pay off debt or save. If all your money is going to interest payments on debt and unnecessary daily expenses, you won't have any to save. If you don't save, you can look forward to a retirement featuring such meals as ramen noodles, Spam, beans and rice, pork and beans, and Alpo.

Why Pay Attention to Spending?

Most personal finance books, including the get-rich-quick books, all want to focus on one side of the household ledger—the earning side. "Get rich in real estate!" "Become a millionaire day-trader!" "Wealth through ostrich farming!"

But how do you accumulate a pile of cash in the first place so you can take advantage of wealth-building advice? You pay attention to spending. In the short term, not spending a buck beats earning a buck every time.

Why Pay Attention to Spending? 1-2-3

1. **Magnitude.** Saved money is more valuable than earned money.
2. **Speed.** Cutting spending is quicker than earning money.
3. **Control.** You can do something about spending today.

These concepts about why spending is important come from my previous book, *Living Rich by Spending Smart*. But they're so fundamental, they bear repeating.

The following descriptions tell you why.

1. Magnitude

You keep 100 cents of an unspent dollar but maybe 60 to 75 cents of an earned one, after taxes, Social Security, and the other deductions take their bite from your paycheck. Cutting out a $50-per-month cable TV bill is the same as a $30,000-a-year worker getting a year's pay raise of 3.3 percent, or $1,000. Benjamin Franklin said, "A penny saved is a penny earned." But that was before the era of income taxes. Today, a saved penny is worth far more than an earned one.

2. Speed

Cutting spending is faster than earning money. You can cancel an expense, such as your gym membership, and start saving money today. You will be instantly better off. But it takes a long time to change your income. It might be months before you can get a pay raise at work, and overtime hours might be sporadically available. The only immediate thing you can do about income is to get a second job that starts this week. Or, as many Americans do, you can use fake income, such as a credit card that gives you an illusion that you have more cash. Of course, that just creates a crisis later on when the credit card bill arrives.

3. Control

You have more control over spending than income. You make dozens of spending decisions a day, from a morning mocha latte at Starbucks to whether you turn up the heat an extra degree in your home. However, your decisions about income are few on a daily basis, outside of resolving to get up and go to work so you aren't fired.

What to Spend Discretionary Money On

Discretionary spending is spending you have choices about. You don't have much choice to pay the mortgage or the electric bill. But you do have choices about a significant portion of your annual spending. It's the coffee and doughnut you buy each morning, the music you download from iTunes, the greens fees for golf, or the extra purse in that color you didn't have.

What to Spend Discretionary Money On, 1-2-3

1. Things you care about.
2. Experiences.
3. Things that rise in value.

1. Things You Care About

Fundamental to the spending smart philosophy is reducing spending on things you don't care about so you can spend that money on things you *do* care about. This might seem elementary. "Isn't that what everybody does?" you might ask.

Not really.

When is the last time you shopped for new home phone service or insurance? Do you really care which

company provides your dial tone or pays your survivors, as long as they provide high-quality service?
Those two examples alone could be worth hundreds of
dollars a year. That's money you could spend on something you need or want.

Think about work lunches. Many people would prefer to eat the delicious leftover meatloaf from last
night's dinner rather than go out to eat. They truly don't
care about eating out for lunch. Paying for that restaurant or cafeteria lunch would be money poorly spent.
Yet, because they didn't get around to packing that
meatloaf sandwich for work, lunch money trickled out
of their lives.

That waste is replicated over and over again, dollar
by dollar, day after day. Soon we're a walking, talking
sieve of money leaks.

Everything has an opportunity cost. Opportunity
cost is what you can't buy because you bought something else. You can't go on the Caribbean vacation
because you refuse to bring lunch to work. It's a trade-
off. It doesn't matter how much money you earn, there
are always trade-offs and opportunity costs. I would
rather trade money spent on stuff I don't care about
and, instead, spend it on stuff I need and want. I bet you
would, too. A sister concept is to measure the *psychological value* from a purchase, or how the purchase
makes you feel. That might seem like an overly touchy-
feely idea. But it's real, nonetheless.

Some people derive a psychological benefit from
having a luxury wristwatch, for example. It might make
them feel a sense of accomplishment or superiority. If

they can afford it, people who get that extra feeling might be spending smarter buying a brand closer to Rolex than Timex. Other people get no psychological boost from the brand of their wristwatch. An expensive watch for them is money poorly spent.

2. Experiences

Did you know you could buy happiness? It's true, if you believe a slew of recent academic research. That research has shown, time and again, that people are happier when spending money on positive life experiences, rather than on things.

The thrill of buying more stuff wears off in short order. By contrast, the longevity of a great memory improves over time. The other component to spending for happiness is including people. Solo experiences, it seems, don't generate near as much joy.

So spend discretionary money on summer vacations and weekend getaways, concerts, board games for the family, and special dinners out (not routine ones).

Experiences appreciate, assets depreciate. Save on the latter to get more of the former.

3. Things That Rise in Value

This is a tough one, but many wealthy people swear by it. It's wiser to spend your money on things that have a chance to go up in value, rather than things that are sure to plummet in value. In other words, try to do more investing than consuming.

The most obvious examples are two of the biggest purchases for any household: a house and a car.

Homes almost always rise in value over the long term. The recent national housing crisis, which saw home prices decline, is an anomaly. So, give the nod to spending on education or sharpening job skills that will lead to a higher salary. Invest in your own business and buy mutual funds. All of those at least have a chance at being worth more in the future than you spent on them. That makes them worthy of consideration.

Of course, you'll have to weed out spending money on get-rich-quick schemes, from the state lottery to pyramid schemes to no-money-down real estate.

QUICK TIP

If someone wants to sell you a program so you can make big money like they're making, pause a moment. Think about it. Why would they put money, time, and energy into developing a tape set or live presentation instead of doing that thing that makes them big money? It's illogical, unless they're truly being charitable. More likely, they make their big money on selling you the false hope of making big money.

By contrast, buying a new car or truck is a lousy investment. It is certain to lose a ton of value the moment you drive away from the car lot. A new car loses about 30 percent of its value in the first year. Most consumer purchases—from new electronic gadgets to muffins in the morning to a new leather jacket—all lose value quickly.

QUICK TIP

When buying something that will depreciate, imagine what you could sell it for at a garage sale the next day. A $15 music CD becomes 75 cents. An $80 cordless phone becomes $6. A $50 toaster oven becomes $5. That puts the purchase in perspective in a hurry.

Of course, we all must buy many things that deteriorate in value. But if you can shift some spending from consuming to investing, you'll be wealthier for it.

Now that we're on the same page philosophically, let's get down to the practical advice.

PART I

Spending Smart Today

Chapter 2

First Things First

Getting Started

You can take a number of supereasy steps to get your financial life in order. For some tasks, it's a matter of actually doing them and crossing them off your list. Others require periodic maintenance.

Often, these fundamentals alone will put you on a path to money success. It's like learning to golf. If you don't have a proper grip and stance, your swing is doomed. Children can't read until they know the alphabet and what sounds letters make. You'll be an unsuccessful driver until you learn about the accelerator, the brake, and the rules of the road.

These fundamentals are always taught—and learned—the same way, step-by-step, in a process as easy as 1-2-3.

Taking Stock

Nobody is starting this minute with a clean financial slate. We already have a lot going on. We're spending and saving every day. So, it's time to take stock.

Taking Stock, 1-2-3

1. **Take a snapshot.** Find out where you stand now.
2. **Look back.** Track previous spending to see where your money goes.
3. **Look ahead.** Set specific goals for where money will go in the future.

Imagine your money life is moving along a timeline. All you own and all you owe is constantly changing, with every swipe of your debit card and every deposit in your retirement plan.

It's important occasionally to take a snapshot of where you are now, a freeze-frame in the motion picture that is your money life.

In the introduction, I wrote about how receiving financial advice is like taking driving directions from a GPS navigation device in your car. No matter how good the machine is, it can't give you directions to where you're going until it knows where you are now. It pinpoints your location by searching for and locking in satellites as it boots up.

Well, it's time to boot up with your finances and find out where you are. It's the first step in getting to where you want to go.

1. Take a Snapshot

There are two simple exercises to hone in on where you are.

First, add up all the money you ever earned in your life. I first saw this task in the book *Your Money or Your Life* by Joe Dominguez and Vicki Robin. The book is great, but the authors go into excruciating detail with this exercise. I think you can get close with just a little effort.

If you have worked for employers your whole career, you can total your lifetime earnings fairly accurately from your annual Social Security statement, which details how much you earned each year. The statement comes a few months before your birthday. If you need a copy, go online to www.socialsecurity.gov/statement to have one mailed to you, or call 1-800-772-1213.

Also, refer to federal income-tax returns. If you've worked at the same employer for a long time, the human resources department probably has a record of your earnings. Estimate other income, such as gifts of money, family loans that were forgiven, money earned as a teenager, even significant gambling winnings.

This trip through your earnings history should be illuminating. It lets you know you have earned significant money over your lifetime. This counters any notion that you don't have enough money to save or enough money to manage.

The second step is to figure out what you're worth today, specifically your net worth. If you liquidated everything in your life—sold everything and paid off all your debts—what would you have to show for it?

Create two columns on paper: all you own (assets) and all you owe (liabilities).

For example, money in your retirement plan is an asset. Furniture and jewelry are assets. Don't stress yourself out trying to get superaccurate values. Just give items ballpark estimates. Meanwhile, credit card debt is a liability, as are student loans and family loans.

If you're making installment payments on something you own, it might be both an asset and a liability. For example, if you own a home with a market value of $300,000, that goes in the assets column. If your mortgage is $225,000, that goes in the liability column. The result? A net $75,000 is added to your net worth. It's similar if you're making car payments, although some people actually owe more than the vehicle is worth. If so, the vehicle actually subtracts from total net worth.

So, now you have two numbers: your total lifetime earnings and your net worth.

The big question to ask yourself is, "With all the working and earning I've done over the years, what do I have to show for it?" A lot, or too little?

Of course, much of that earned money went to necessities that added little or nothing directly to your net worth—food, clothing, vacations. Meanwhile, some of your assets have appreciated, such as your retirement plan or the value of your house.

If you're still in your working years and your net worth roughly equals your lifetime earnings, you're doing really well. Even if your net worth is a quarter to a half of your lifetime earnings, you're not in bad shape.

The ratio should improve to one-to-one or better as you approach retirement, says Liz Pulliam Weston in *Easy Money: How to Simplify Your Finances and Get What You Want Out of Life*.

But if your net worth is zero or negative, you might honestly ask and answer, "With all I've earned, what do I have to show for it? Nothing."

The big question is, "Now that you have a snapshot of where you are with money, what will you do from here?" Will you do things to add to your net worth, such as save and invest? Or, will you buy more consumer goods and services, which subtracts from your net worth? After 10 more years of earning money, will you have more to show for it than during the past 10?

A wealth formula from the best-selling book *The Millionaire Next Door* provides an interesting exercise. It offers a measuring stick for how well you are accumulating wealth.

Net worth = your age times your income, divided by 10.

A 40-year-old with a household income of $60,000 should have a net worth of $240,000. And that's just to be what the authors called an "average accumulator of wealth," AAW. To be what the authors called a PAW, prodigious accumulator of wealth, you'll need twice that much net worth.

A basic philosophy is one often attributed to American philosopher Bill Earle: "If your outgo exceeds your income, then your upkeep will be your downfall."

2. Look Back

Now that you've explored your earnings compared with your wealth, let's turn to spending. Minding your spending isn't a substitute for trying to raise your income. You still need to do that. But, as I highlighted previously, spending is where you have the most control right away.

The best way to get a handle on spending is to track it. I'm not talking about doing a full-fledged budget. Instead, just track your expenses and categorize them.

Start by tracking expenses for two months. It doesn't matter how you do it. You can use pencil and paper, a spreadsheet, or software programs such as Quicken or Microsoft Money. You can keep a notepad with you at all times to jot down spending, or compile store receipts with monthly bills less often. If you mostly use debit and credit cards instead of cash, a convenient list of transactions will be on your statements.

Then categorize the expenses. Use categories that fit your spending. Attempt to get a little detail on big expenditures, such as food. Split it into two subcategories, groceries and dining out.

QUICK TIP

Several Web sites now offer to help you track spending. Among the most popular is Mint.com, which is free and worth considering. It can automatically import transactions from many bank accounts, credit card, and investment accounts. It also suggests vendors that could save you money. Similar sites are Wesabe.com, Yodlee.com, Buxfer.com, and Geezeo.com.

With these categorized totals in hand, this is where you face the ugly reality that you spend $534 a month on dining out or that, on average, you spend $156 a month on shoes. You're probably already familiar with your once-a-month expenses, such as your electric bill and car payment. The more shocking figures will be the little money leaks that add up. "Do I really spend $50 a month on bottled water, $40 a month in bank fees, and $60 a month on DVD movies?"

The point is to identify where your money has been misspent in the past so you can redirect it toward your priorities in the future. How do you know if it's been misspent? That's the beauty. You decide.

3. Look Ahead

"Speaking of priorities, how do I get myself a set of those?"

You set spending goals.

As the saying goes, "If you aim at nothing, you will hit it every time." Abraham Lincoln said, "A goal properly set is halfway reached." And Benjamin E. Mays, a mentor to Martin Luther King Jr., said, "It must be borne in mind that the tragedy of life does not lie in not reaching your goal. The tragedy of life lies in having no goal to reach."

"Yeah, yeah, yeah," you might be thinking. "Set goals. Next chapter, please!"

Before you dismiss the importance of setting goals about money, read on.

Goals give you direction and can provide peace of mind. They even have application in daily life. With all the marketing bombarding us every day and fueling our wants, a set of goals help us to say no. They remind us there's something we want more than the tempting purchase right in front of us.

So, the antidote for leaky, undisciplined spending is having goals.

Developing spending goals is not difficult. Brainstorm the big, expensive stuff you want to buy and do. Write them down, both long-term goals and short-term ones. The only rules are that each objective must have two components, a dollar figure and a date for completion. We'll talk about some of these in-depth during future chapters, but the following are some typical goals:

- **Eliminate consumer debt.** Everybody knows you want to get rid of debt so you can stop paying interest. But some of the most valuable benefits are nonfinancial—less money stress, a sense of freedom, and possibly more relationship harmony with your significant other. High-interest credit card debt should be an urgent priority. Mortgage debt and low-interest student loans are a lower priority to pay off quickly.
- **Build an emergency fund.** Creating a rainy-day fund can be a two-step process. The long-term goal is a fund equal to three to six months worth of bare-bones living expenses, such as food, shelter, and utilities. A shorter-term goal might be to stash away $1,000 or $2,500. Then, it's not a crisis or a time to incur debt when the car needs new tires at the same time the roof needs repairs.

- **Buy a house.** Be clear about what price you will pay for a house, which lets you estimate an amount for a down payment. If you're already a homeowner, perhaps you desire a vacation home. If so, it is unlikely to become a reality unless you begin planning for it.

- **Take a vacation.** Vacations are optional, but don't totally dismiss the value of shared experiences with family and friends. Paid-for vacations are better. I recall a *Parade* magazine cartoon that showed a couple sitting on lounge chairs aboard a cruise ship. Suntan lotion and an umbrella drink rested beside them. The guy turns to his wife and says, "This would be a lot more relaxing if we could afford it."

- **Complete home fix-ups.** For homeowners, list your major home-improvement projects and home-furnishing purchases in priority order.

- **Buy a vehicle.** You will replace your car or truck. It's just a matter of when. Start talking about the type of vehicle you might get next and when. That should give you ample time to start saving a substantial down payment, or better yet, to pay in cash. A slightly used car is a better value than buying new.

- **Retire.** Past generations often had defined pensions, the kind where they guarantee you a check every month regardless of what the financial markets are doing. But, today, it's your job to figure out how to squirrel away hundreds of thousands, and maybe millions, of dollars, before you quit work. What type of retirement do you foresee? And when do you expect to gear down your working life? Where will you be living in retirement? Do you anticipate knocking off work at age 70 and being a homebody or quitting at age 55 and traveling the world? Those plans require vastly different amounts of retirement savings. Run through scenarios with easy-to-use calculators online at such sites as Dinkytown.com or ChooseToSave.org. Estimate the nest egg you'll need. From that, you can back into a single dollar figure: the amount you should be saving each month for the type of retirement you want.

- **Kids' college.** Although important, saving for kids' college expenses is a lower priority than most. You can often get a low-interest loan for college expenses, but nobody lends money for retirement, for example. Open a 529 savings plan and start contributing regularly, even if it's only $50 a month. As you free up money in your life, revisit this goal and raise your contributions. Few families will be able to fund all their other savings goals and save 100 percent of college tuition. Do what you can. Learn more about college savings plans online at Savingforcollege.com.

Establishing goals is only the start. The rest is follow-through. Allocate regular and automatic savings amounts toward each goal that needs to be started now. We'll talk more about that in the chapters ahead.

If the goal amounts seem intimidating, break it down further. For example, don't think of saving $2,500 for an emergency fund. Instead, you're saving $6.85 per day for a year. Opening separate fee-free savings accounts for some top goals, such as a car fund, can help improve your focus on the goal. Set up an automatic draft from your checking account to fund each goal. Your money is finite, so you might have to delay funding lower-priority goals until ones that are more important—or more immediate—are either under way or completed.

You should also keep close track of your progress toward achieving the goals, regularly revising both the dollar figures—upward, we hope—and time frames—sooner, we hope.

Then, next time you're tempted with an impulse purchase, you'll have a reason to say no. That's fundamental to spending smart.

Estate Planning

Nobody wants to consider their own demise, but death planning is part of being an adult.

Estate Planning, 1-2-3

Make an appointment with an estate-planning attorney to draw up or update the following documents:

1. **Will.**
2. **Durable power of attorney for finances and for health care.**
3. **Living will (pull-the-plug papers).**

"Isn't this a book about saving money?" you might be thinking. "Why is he telling me to pay an attorney to draw up these documents?"

You could use lower-cost alternatives, certainly. You can try to write a will yourself with the help of books. You can write it with the help of a computer software program. In fact, a program called Quicken WillMaker Plus by Nolo generally gets rave reviews. You could buy the Will & Trust Kit sold by personal finance guru Suze Orman or use such Web sites as itsmylife.com and LegalZoom.com.

But sometimes it just makes sense to cough up the money and make sure it's done right. This is one of those times. Consider the issues: Who gets your money if you die, who gets your kids if you die, who's going to pay the bills if you're physically unable, and should doctors keep you on artificial life support?

Rules vary by state on this stuff. For example, do you know how many witnesses to the signing of a will your state requires? If your life is the least bit complicated—for example, estranged family members, blended families, a special-needs child—these documents become all the more important. A good attorney will walk you through all the scenarios, including many you might not have thought about.

In short, spending a few hundred dollars for an estate-planning attorney to create these documents is spending smart. There's no magic way of choosing an attorney. Your state bar association will certainly have a list. But you might ask for recommendations from friends, relatives, and other professionals you use, such as an accountant.

1. Will

A will is often the centerpiece of estate planning. Wills aren't only for rich people. A will dictates who gets your money and property if you die. It dictates who will care for your minor children. If you die without a will, the state decides.

If you're married, you might think it's simple: Everything—the house, money, and kids—goes to your spouse. But what if you both die at the same time? Think car crash. It's not so clear-cut.

If you're paying by the hour with an attorney, you can save money by talking through some scenarios and making decisions before you enter the law firm's offices. If you have children, you need to pick a guardian. You'll need to decide on an executor of the estate, which is the person who manages the assets right after you die. List your assets and liabilities and decide which beneficiary gets which asset.

If you already have a will created years ago, whether by an attorney, software program, or some other way, it might be worth having an attorney review it again, especially if your life circumstances have changed significantly since the will was drafted.

QUICK TIP

This estate-planning move is absolutely free. Make sure all your financial accounts have up-to-date primary and secondary beneficiaries. These accounts include retirement plans, bank accounts, and life insurance policies.

---

2. Durable Power of Attorney for Finances and for Health Care

If you're incapacitated, you'll need someone to make decisions about your money and your medical treatment. These are really different issues and can be different people, but you should proactively decide who it should be in both cases. These documents are generally part of a package of estate-planning documents an attorney will draw up for you.

3. Living Will

A living will addresses the scenario that, for some, might be worse than death. You're being kept alive artificially, being fed through tubes and your quality of life has diminished to near nothing. What type of end-of-life care do you want if you're terminally ill or incapacitated?

Do You Need a Living Trust?

There's nothing wrong with a revocable living trust, which is often touted as an alternative or supplement to a will. This legal document allows you to transfer assets into a trust while you're living, which can help bypass the court process called probate after you die. It might save money on legal and court fees during probate—which is expensive in some states, such as California—and make the process quicker and more private.

But living trusts are oversold and cost much more to prepare than a will. A lawyer-prepared will might cost $300, whereas a living trust might cost $3,000, although you can prepare a trust yourself. Trusts also require more maintenance than a will. For example, you have to transfer everything you own—personal property you have now and will buy in the future—into the trust. That can be a lot of paperwork, both when setting up the trust and going forward.

If you're considering a trust, have a good reason to get one. What is the cost now, and what are your heirs likely to save later, when you die? And again, if you want a trust, consider having it drawn up by an attorney, instead of a salesperson selling boilerplate trusts.

Identity Theft

Identity theft is when someone illegally uses your personal information, such as a Social Security number or credit card number, usually for financial gain.

Most important about the advice here is what *not* to do. For example, unless you've been a victim of identity theft, you don't need to pay for credit monitoring. Monitor your credit yourself by accessing your credit reports for free, as we'll talk about in Chapter 6, "Credit When Credit's Due."

Nobody needs to pay for identity theft insurance, which just reimburses you for incidental costs of cleaning up identity theft. It might reimburse you for the costs of mailings and phone calls, and perhaps lost wages and attorney fees. But few victims of identity theft actually incur any out-of-pocket expenses.

Instead, focus on these three, simple steps to help prevent identity theft.

Identity Theft, 1-2-3

1. **Be guarded.** Think twice about divulging personal information.
2. **Buy a crosscut shredder.** Shred mail and documents containing personal information.
3. **Opt out.** Stop credit card solicitations by going online to OptOutPrescreen.com.

These three steps are easy and relatively inexpensive, especially compared to some of the pricey identity-theft products and services out there.

1. Be Guarded

This might seem like obvious advice, but it's by far the most important. The most dangerous type of identity theft is when a thief opens a new credit account in your name. When this happens, it's often because a thief has your Social Security number. So, don't give out your number unless there's a good reason. For example, it seems every doctor's office wants you to fill out a bunch of paperwork, which often includes your Social Security number—it seems, as a matter of routine. I usually just leave it blank or provide the last four digits of my number. I've never had a problem. If you try that and the doctor's office insists on getting the full number, at least get a good explanation as to why.

Less obvious might be safeguarding your information by using fewer personal checks. Think about it. A check has your name, address, and bank routing number. That's everything a thief would need to empty your account. Instead, pay by credit card and electronic payments. And if you must write a check that you will mail, avoid putting it in your mailbox for pickup. A thief might pluck it out of your box before the postal worker does.

2. Buy a Crosscut Shredder

You should be able to find a good shredder for less than $50. The finer the confetti it makes, the better. Avoid ribbon shredders that cut into long strips. Those pieces can be reassembled by a thief.

Regularly shred all credit card offers, so a thief doesn't pick an application out of your trash and steal your identity. Shred documents that list both your name and account number, especially your Social Security number.

3. Opt Out

Stop many unsolicited credit offers by visiting www.OptOutPrescreen.com or calling 1-888-5-OPTOUT. This will help prevent a thief from stealing a credit card application from your mailbox and signing up for a card. You can opt out for five years online or permanently by mail using a form available at the Web site.

While you're at it, opt out of junk mail at www.dma-choice.org. You must renew after five years. And stop unwanted catalogs at www.catalogchoice.org. You'll reduce paper waste and save a few trees, while reducing unnecessary spending temptations.

And post your telephone number on the National Do-Not-Call Registry run by the Federal Trade Commission. Sign up online at www.donotcall.gov or call 1-888-382-1222.

For more ways to reduce junk mail, see "Fact Sheet 4: Reducing Junk Mail at the Privacy Rights Clearinghouse," at www.privacyrights.org.

What about Fraud Alerts and Credit Freezes?

Many people try to safeguard their credit files as an identity-theft prevention measure, hoping to thwart thieves attempting to open new credit accounts in their name. Two of the main tools are fraud alerts and credit freezes.

In short, fraud alerts are a waste of time. Credit freezes are great if you think you might be at risk for identity theft.

Fraud Alerts

Fraud alerts are red flags in your credit file. They are notations that suggest a creditor should double-check the identity of the person applying for credit.

You can place fraud alerts on your credit reports for free by contacting a credit bureau. Ideally, you should only need to contact one of the three. It is supposed to forward the request to the other bureaus. However, evidence shows that this doesn't happen all the time. So, if you're going to place fraud alerts on your credit files, contact all three bureaus:

- TransUnion: 1-800-680-7289
- Equifax: 1-800-525-6285
- Experian: 1-888-397-3742

Use your cell phone number as the fraud-alert contact number. That way, if you're applying for credit, the creditor can call to confirm your identity quickly, no matter where you are.

However, there are problems with fraud alerts. First, alerts expire every 90 days. So, you need to continually renew fraud-alert requests. This is essentially what the heavily advertised LifeLock and similar services do for you.

Second, creditors are not required to double-check identity just because there's a fraud alert on file. It's merely a suggestion. So, your effort might be wasted.

Alerts were meant to be used by victims of identity theft. However, because consumers can place free 90-day alerts on their credit files, many people implemented fraud alerts as a preventative measure—again, some through services such as

LifeLock. As a result, fraud alerts became useless because many creditors ignored the warnings. It's like the fabled boy who cried wolf. So, often, the alert didn't really signify a potential identity theft. After a while, creditors started ignoring the warning.

Third, you might have a hassle getting on-the-spot credit, not only for credit card applications, but also for signing up for a wireless phone plan, for example. If the creditor pays attention to the fraud alert, it will contact you before approving the application.

Credit Freezes

A credit security freeze is far more restrictive than a fraud alert. If you place a freeze on your reports, no creditor can access your credit file until you "thaw" it—provide permission by supplying a personal identification number that unlocks the reports. Unlike an alert, freezes don't expire every 90 days. Most freezes are permanent until you lift them, whereas others are good for seven years. For state-specific information on security freezes, go online to FinancialPrivacyNow.org.

The distinction between fraud alerts and credit security freezes is the difference between a burglar alarm and an impenetrable door lock. One tells you to worry about a thief; the other never allows the thief in.

But, there are hassles. Most people have to pay a fee every time they freeze their credit and again when they thaw it. A typical fee is $10 per credit bureau, or $30 to place a freeze with all three bureaus.

And, your credit is locked down tight. So, you won't get on-the-spot credit until you thaw it. That also means a potential employer might not be able to run a credit check until you thaw your credit, at least with the bureau that it uses. This delay problem seems to be getting better, however. In late 2008, the credit bureaus were lifting freezes in about 15 minutes, instead of the three business days called for in many state statutes.

If I had a reason to believe my personal information was compromised, I would use a credit freeze. Or if it helps you sleep at night, go for it. Otherwise, I wouldn't bother. Again, a fraud alert is pretty useless. Don't bother. And definitely don't pay any company to place fraud alerts for you.

Banking

Not that many years ago, you would choose a bank from the few available in your town or city. You visited the bank and filled out paperwork to open new checking and savings accounts. To become a member of a consumer-friendly credit union, you had to work for an employer affiliated with that credit union.

Today, things are far different. For one, the choices are so much broader. You can choose among hundreds of banks across the country. You can open an account by filling out forms on the Internet and electronically transferring money into the account, which isn't as difficult as it sounds.

As for credit unions, most people nowadays qualify for at least one.

No matter what accounts you investigate, keep one main criterion in mind: No fees! Or as few as possible. You shouldn't have to pay a bank to hold your money. The implied deal is this: They get use of your money. In return, you get use of a bank account and some meager amount of interest. Obviously, a fee for bouncing a check is reasonable. But so many others just aren't.

Here's a generalization that will draw criticism, but it's true most of the time: The huge national banking behemoths are probably not the right bank for you, or any consumer. The fees are likely to be numerous and expensive, and the service is likely to be lousy. And as we saw with all the bank failures and bailouts during the financial crisis of 2008 and 2009, big banks are certainly no safer.

Get the Bank Accounts You Need, 1-2-3

1. **Get a no-fee checking account.**
2. **Set up at least one high-interest online bank account.**
3. **Join a credit union.**

1. Get a No-Fee Checking Account

Checking accounts are probably your most important account. A checking account is your command center, where all the action is. Money is coming in and going out every week. It's also where you can get ripped off with a plethora of bank fees. So, it's important to get a suitable account that's not going to cost you money.

When the first priority is to limit fees, make sure you get a free checking account, which means no monthly charge and no minimum balance, unless you're certain you can regularly meet that minimum balance requirement. You should also have unlimited check writing and free use of your debit card, whether you use a PIN code or sign a sales slip. You can even find accounts that don't charge ATM fees for using the wrong bank's teller machine. Others will rebate a certain dollar amount each month for using "foreign" ATMs.

Here are criteria you might judge a bank on, when it comes to checking accounts:

- Online bill paying
- Interest on balances
- Overdraft protection
- Unlimited check writing
- Free linked accounts
- 24-hour automated banking
- Free or discounted check printing
- Nonbank ATM fee rebates
- E-mail alerts
- Debit rewards card
- Downloads to Quicken or Microsoft Money
- Mobile banking services

As of this writing, a new online tool can help. It's at FindABetterBank.com. There, you answer questions about which features of a checking account are important to you. The Web site suggests a bank for you. Bankrate.com, a generally good financial Web site, also has a tool for choosing a checking account.

Try not to fixate on getting an interest-bearing checking account, at least when interest rates are so low, as they have been for years. Even if a bank paid a healthy 2 percent on checking, that's only $30 in interest per year on an average balance of $1,500. Fees could quickly demolish any interest earnings. Besides, banks regularly change the interest rates they pay on accounts, so it shouldn't be your highest priority.

Rewards Checking

If you're the type of person who must make the most interest you can, you can try a rewards checking account, which pays about 6 percent interest on balances up to $25,000 and offers free online bill paying and no ATM fees. But there are catches. The primary requirement is you have to make 10 debit-card purchases per month. Not only that, but you must also use your card as a credit card in which you sign for the purchase, instead of using a PIN code. You also have to create at least one direct deposit into the account and receive an electronic statement instead of a paper one.

How can banks afford to pay such a higher rate of interest? Banks clean up on merchant fees for signature-based debit-card transactions, so they share that with you in the form of a higher interest rate. Compare rewards checking accounts at HighYieldCheckingDeals.com and CheckingFinder.com.

Because checking accounts are so integral to your financial life, switching accounts can be a headache. That's especially true if you have a number of automatic deposits and bills paid directly from your checking account. To help, many banks are offering switch kits, which provide some hand-holding through the process of opening the new account and closing the old one.

Is it worth changing checking accounts? Look back at all the fees you paid over the past year. The size of that dollar figure will tell you.

Figure 2.1 shows averages for some of the most common checking-account fees.

$2: Most common ATM surcharge

$28.95: Average bounced check fee

$11.97: Average monthly service fee on interest-bearing accounts

$3,461.84: Average balance needed to avoid fees on interest-bearing accounts
Source: Bankrate.com survey 2008

FIGURE 2.1   *Checking-account fees by the numbers*

BANKING QUICK TIPS

- *Fee-free cash. If you can't find an in-network ATM, look for a nearby supermarket that will give you cash back on debit-card transactions. Buy something small that you would have bought anyway. Make the purchase using your debit card, enter the PIN code and get your cash fee-free.*

- *Cheap checks. Instead of ordering books of checks through your bank for $25, order them online for less than $10. See Walmartchecks.com, Checksinthemail.com, CheckWorks.com, and Checksunlimited.com.*

---

2. Set Up at Least One High-Interest Online Bank Account

This is where you might want to keep your emergency fund, next-car fund, and other short-term savings. See Chapter 7, "How to Save Money," for strategic ways to use these accounts.

The idea is to earn a little interest while the money is parked for a relatively short time, for example, less than five years. That's as opposed to investing, where the goal is long-term growth of the money.

You might want to set up more than one savings account, each earmarked for a specific purpose. I have one for an emergency fund and one for home improvements, for example.

Good advice on savings is easy: Shop by rate as long as the bank is insured by the Federal Deposit Insurance Corp. (FDIC). However, you should determine whether it's an introductory rate that drops quickly after a certain number of months.

The highest rates are offered in money market accounts and online-only banks. Bankrate.com has a robust list. If you don't want to do research from scratch, go with EmigrantDirect.com, INGdirect.com, or HSBCdirect.com. These online-only banks regularly have among the highest savings rates in the country.

A minor drawback of these savings accounts is you must transfer money into and out of the accounts electronically, which isn't as scary as it sounds. It's basically providing a bank routing number, which is one of the groups of numbers on the bottom of your paper checks. The drawback is that it could take a couple of business days for the transfer of money to go through. In most scenarios where you'll be depositing and withdrawing money from a savings account, that shouldn't be a problem.

FDIC Rules: Is My Money Safe?

It's unusual, but banks can fail, as we now know all too well after the financial crisis. However, if the bank is FDIC insured, your money is safe up to $100,000[1] per person on the account at a single institution. If an account is held jointly by a husband and a wife, they each are insured for $100,000, for a total of $200,000.

If you have a lot of money to sock in an account, a good strategy is to deposit about $90,000 per person per bank. That way, your principal of $90,000 plus its interest will be insured. Certain retirement accounts are insured up to $250,000 per owner, per insured bank.

For more information, see fdic.gov/consumers.

There's so much competition among banks, there's no reason to get an account without FDIC deposit insurance.

3. Join a Credit Union

Credit unions might be the perfect mix of favorable rates and personal service. Credit unions, which are not-for-profit, can offer good rates because customers are the shareholders. Credit unions are affiliated groups of people who pool their money and lend it to each other. Unlike banks, they don't have divided loyalties—trying to serve a customer at the same time as boosting profits and the stock price for shareholders.

Credit unions are exempt from paying federal income taxes, which allows them to be very competitive, despite being much smaller than the megabanks. Of course, that makes the banking industry very grumpy. It claims those advantages allow large credit unions to compete unfairly with traditional banks. But the advantages can be a boon for consumers.

Traditionally, the major catch was qualifying for membership in a credit union, through your employer, for example. But nowadays, more people than ever are likely to qualify to join at least one credit union—and probably qualify for several. A 1998 law loosened membership requirements for credit unions. So you might qualify just because you live in a certain county or are a member of a certain church. To find out whether you qualify to join a credit union, ask your employer or family members who belong to a credit union, or go online to credit union search sites, such as FindACreditUnion.com and www.ncua.gov/index-data.html.

Most credit unions require a small savings-account deposit—not a fee—to join. It could be as low as $5 for a lifetime membership. That means you retain membership even if you leave the employer, geographic region, or association that qualified you to be a member.

Credit unions are probably best for borrowing. Auto loans tend to be a great deal, and credit unions might be the only place you can get a personal loan. But you might find the credit union is a good answer for checking and savings, too. Credit union deposits are protected by the National Credit Union Administration with the same protections as FDIC-insured deposits at banks.

Bill Paying

Now that we've gotten some big-picture stuff out of the way, let's drill down to the daily logistics of handling money—more specifically, paying the bills. The first rule of bill paying should go without saying. It is, well, to pay your bills. If you've ever been slapped with a late fee, you know how punitive they can be. And nowadays, missing payments can damage your credit rating, which can make life more expensive in a wide host of ways. So, pay your bills on time, every time.

That said, we can move on to *how* you pay bills.

The usual bill-paying process—waiting for a bill to arrive, writing a check, and mailing off the payment—is one of the worst methods of paying bills today. The old method is more expensive, more hassle, and more susceptible to fraud and identity theft.

In short, efficient bill paying means moving from pen and paper to keyboard and computer.

Bill Paying, 1-2-3

1. **Use direct deposit.**
2. **Automate bill paying.**
3. **Prioritize in a crisis.**

1. Use Direct Deposit

If you automate nothing else, at least have your paychecks and other regular income, such as Social Security payments, deposited automatically into a bank account. It cuts down on the time and hassle of going to a bank or teller machine. And you don't have to worry about misplacing the check. Most important, it gets money into your account quickly, which could help you avoid fees for overdrafts.

If you work for an employer, your human resources or payroll department can probably help you get signed up for direct deposit. You'll need the bank-routing number for the account you want money deposited into.

2. Automate Bill Paying

You can use three main ways to pay bills automatically. Not only will you ensure bills are paid on time, you avoid the hassle and expense of checks, envelopes, and postage. The average consumer pays 11.5 bills per month, according to a survey by Harris Interactive and the Marketing Workshop. And we Americans spend about 22 hours a year paying bills, according to the U.S. Bureau of Labor Statistics.

The first way to pay automatically is for trusted payees, such as your mortgage company. And you don't even have to use the Internet. Set up an automatic monthly withdrawal, or debit, from your checking account. You supply the checking-account number and the payee automatically withdraws money when the bill is due.

You'll have peace of mind knowing that important bills are being paid—your lights won't go dark because you lost the electric bill. If you're wary of direct debit, dip your toe in the water by putting one bill on auto-debit—your mortgage or cable TV bill, for example. Once you see how easy and safe it is, you'll want to put as many of your recurring payments on automatic debit as you can. Of course, you must make sure there's enough money in the account when this withdrawal is made or face insufficient funds penalties. Maintain a cash cushion in your checking account and sign up for overdraft protection. That's where a bank links your checking account to a savings account, line of credit, or credit card. Overdrafts, if they occur, are automatically funded by these other accounts, avoiding a costly overdraft penalty.

The second way to pay a recurring bill is with a credit card, if the vendor will let you. This can be especially good when bills are charged to a rewards credit card, which pays you back a small percentage of your purchases in the form of cash, airline miles, merchandise, or other perks. See Chapter 6 for details. Automatic charges to a credit card are also good for merchants you don't fully trust. That's because credit cards offer more robust consumer protections than direct-bank debits do if a dispute arises.

A big caveat with this method, however, is this: If you don't use credit cards wisely, meaning you pay off the balance every month with no exceptions, don't use this method. You'll end up paying far more in interest charges than the convenience is worth.

Automation Drawbacks

A problem with automating your financial life is the curse of recurring payments. That involves regular charges for products and services you don't want or need anymore. They include gym membership, video-rental club, wine-of-the-month club, satellite-radio subscription, and premium TV channels. Because those payments are automated, it's easy to do nothing and be needlessly charged month after month for services you don't use. Even if the payment is automatic, continue to review your bills monthly and evaluate whether discretionary expenses are worthwhile.

Similarly, you could become complacent about checking monthly bills for errors. And if you switch checking accounts, you'll have to reset automated debits. An expiring credit card might mean you need to provide a biller with a new expiration date, although card companies have programs that allow participating merchants to automatically get new expiration dates.

The third way of automatically paying bills is a little less automatic: Using the Internet to proactively pay a bill. Online bill paying takes a couple of different forms, but each involves electronically authorizing money transfers to a merchant. Some people like it more than automatic debit because they feel like they have more control over what gets paid and when. And it's a good method for infrequent payments.

You could log on to your own bank's Web site and direct the bank to make an electronic payment to a vendor, such as your power company. You would have to repeat this each month for each vendor, although often you can set up repeating payments for fixed-amount bills. Many banks offer online bill paying as a free service.

Another way is to log on to a vendor's Web site to pay your bill. You would pay by typing in a bank account or credit card number. You would have to do this each month and visit a variety of different vendor Web sites, such as the power company, the phone company, and the mortgage company. That's less convenient than a one-stop bill-paying service.

Be sure to sign up for e-mail reminders about when bills are due, a service offered by some merchants.

If automatic bill paying and electronic payments just aren't your style, you could continue the old-fashioned way with some modifications. First, you have to stay especially organized, knowing when payments are due and regularly going through your bills, which you should keep in a predetermined place. To avoid late charges, you could pay each bill as it comes in. Any bank-account interest you forfeit by paying early is relatively minor compared with a potential late charge.

Of course, you'll probably end up using a combination of these bill-paying methods, but the more you can automate, the better. The important thing is to have a reliable, low-hassle system.

3. Prioritize in a Crisis

At one time or another, most people have been caught in a situation where there's too much month left at the end of the money. Job loss, divorce, unexpected auto repairs, or a variety of other untoward financial strikes could derail the best intentions.

During these times of stress, people can get so upset at their money woes that they lose perspective about who should get paid and who shouldn't.

Here are the most important bills to pay: food, shelter, utilities, and transportation. Take care of those, and you can take a deep breath. They are your four pillars of security. Clothing is a necessity, too, but most people can get by temporarily with what they already have. Health insurance is also especially important, as is childcare for some working parents.

Notice credit card companies are not on the list. But make no mistake, card collectors will scream the loudest to get their money. They will try to rattle you during confrontational phone calls, hoping you will divert to them money that should go to your four pillars of security. Keep your cool. Yes, you owe money. But payments for credit card bills, medical bills, and personal loans can wait. Place student loans on hardship deferral.

Of course, you'll damage your creditworthiness for not paying all your bills. But during a money crisis, you need to take care of necessities first so you live to fight another day.

Endnotes

1. On October 3, 2008, Congress temporarily increased FDIC deposit insurance from $100,000 to $250,000 per depositor through December 31, 2009. As of this writing, it is uncertain whether the raised limit will become permanent. Learn more at www.fdic.gov.

Chapter 3

Get FIT (Food, Insurance, Telecommunications)

In *Living Rich by Spending Smart*, I talked about becoming financially FIT, which stands for food, insurance, and telecommunications. These are perfect areas to start a spending makeover because they involve tremendous spending and waste for the average household. An American family of four spends about $14,000 a year in these three areas alone.

These areas are also great for spending cuts because you can save money painlessly. It's not about deprivation. It's about spending smarter, so you can redirect money to things you truly care about. They are the best examples of spending smart.

These are also areas of repeat spending. That means you'll be spending in these areas—food, insurance, and telecommunications—over and over again, every year of your life.

In this chapter, I try to hone in on the absolute best strategies to save you the most money—to make sure you're on your way to becoming financially FIT.

Food at Home

I call this category "food" at home, but I'm really talking about supermarket shopping. So, that includes paper goods, such as napkins and toilet tissue. It includes razor blades, shampoo, and other grooming products. It includes some over-the-counter medications you might pick up at the supermarket.

Food at Home, 1-2-3

1. **Maintain a price list.**
2. **Stockpile sale items.**
3. **Match coupons to sales.**

1. Maintain a Price List

You can't save money at the supermarket unless you can identify a good deal. The problem is that you buy so many items during a shopping trip that it's difficult to remember more than just a few prices.

- Is $2 a box a good price for Cheerios breakfast cereal?
- Is $1 each a great deal for Duracell AA alkaline batteries?
- Is 2 for $6 a bargain on Oscar Mayer Bacon?

The solution is to maintain a price list. A price list is just a simple list of items you buy regularly. A price list helps you spot unadvertised sales. It helps identify fake sales—"sale" items at the end of the supermarket aisle that are really at regular prices or only lightly discounted.

It might also reveal sales cycles for a particular item. In general, sales recur roughly every 12 weeks.

You can use anything from a small-ringed notepad to spreadsheet printouts to a personal digital assistant (PDA) to keep the list. Use whatever you're comfortable with. Set up several columns: store, item, brand, price, and unit size (pounds, ounces, sheets per roll). You might also want to note the date. Four-year-old prices aren't very helpful. As you expand the list, you might want to rearrange it into categories, such as meat, dairy, and beverages.

Don't bother noting one-time purchases or items you seldom buy. At first, just stick to items you use every week. You can always expand the list from there. The only way a price list works is if it's not too time consuming. After just a few weeks, you'll have a pretty good price list assembled, and it will start paying dividends.

The point is to have a benchmark for what a good price is.

Is Organic Food Worth the Price?

As food prices rise, consumers might find it tough to pay premium prices for organic products. But you can save money if you're smart about buying organics.

Organic means the food is produced without pesticides, chemical fertilizers, or antibiotics and generally emphasizes using renewable resources and conserving soil and water. Consumers frequently buy organic food for environmental reasons and because they consider it to be more healthful.

Organic produce typically costs 25 percent to 100 percent more than nonorganic. Especially in challenging economic times, that has consumers reexamining their choices. Here are some do's and don'ts when trying to save money on organic food:

- **Don't settle for "natural."** The term *natural* on packaging has a lot less meaning than *organic*, a term highly regulated by the Department of Agriculture. Don't pay extra for something called *natural* or *all natural*.

- **Do pay for some fruits and vegetables.** It's worth paying more for organic versions of some fruits and vegetables that retain pesticide residue, even after you wash them. Pay for organic versions of peaches, apples, sweet bell peppers, celery, nectarines, strawberries, cherries, pears, grapes, spinach, lettuce, and potatoes, according to the Environmental Working Group, a nonprofit organic research group.

- **Don't pay more for fruits and vegetables with thicker skins that have far less pesticide residue.** You can skip organic onions, avocados, sweet corn, pineapples, mango, asparagus, sweet peas, kiwi, bananas, cabbage, broccoli, and papaya.

- **Do buy organic protein-rich foods.** Meats, poultry, eggs, and dairy products are worth buying as organics because they are free of pesticides, synthetic growth hormones, and antibiotics.

- **Don't buy highly processed organics.** Breads, oils, potato chips, pasta, cereals, and other packaged foods, such as canned or dried fruit and vegetables, are probably not worth buying as organics unless price is no object, *Consumer Reports* said. Much of the health benefit has been processed out.

- **Do buy organic baby food.** Baby food tends to be made from condensed fruits and vegetables, some of which might contain pesticides. Or make your own baby food from organic whole fruits and vegetables.

- **Do buy local.** You can find organic food from local farmers' markets and local producers.

- **Do try store brands.** More supermarkets and large discounters, such as Wal-Mart, are offering private-label organics, which are cheaper than name brands.

- **Do use coupons.** Look for coupons for organic products in the Sunday newspaper or go online to the free coupon database at CouponMom.com and enter the search term "organic." Get coupons directly from organic producers' Web sites and sign up for their e-mail newsletters, which contain coupons. Examples are OrganicValley.com, SCOjuice.com, ColemanNatural.com, and Stonyfield.com. The site Healthesavers.com has printable coupons for some organic products.

- **Do grow your own.** If you are the gardening type and have a back yard, grow your own vegetables and receive the side benefits of exercise and a regular hobby.

For more information, see GreenerChoices.org, FoodNews.org, and OrganicConsumers.org.

2. Stockpile Sale Items

This gets to the heart of the spending smart strategy on groceries: Each week, don't buy what you need. Instead, buy what's on sale, and stock up.

This cherry-picking strategy sounds simple enough, but it has a few moving parts.

- **Loyalty cards.** In most supermarkets, you'll have to sign up for a store loyalty card to qualify for sale prices. Supermarkets nowadays don't typically have sales that apply to everyone. Make no mistake: The supermarket is tracking your purchasing habits. That might give you the willies. But in the end, it's doubtful that anyone will ever examine what you were buying. And who cares?

Someone could follow you around the store—a public place—and collect the same information. Anyway, a loyalty card is often the only way to qualify for sale prices, and shopping the sales is your best weapon to lowering your food spending.

- **Sales flyers.** Examine the weekly sales flyers for advertised specials. They often come in the newspaper or by mail. You can also go online to mygrocerydeals.com, which has digital versions of many sales flyers. Pay special attention to what's advertised on the front and back covers. They are likely to be *loss leaders*, meaning the store is selling them so cheaply they're actually losing money. They hope to attract buyers into the store to purchase more high-profit items, which compensates for the loss leaders. I'm not going to tell you how to plan your meals, but if you can plan dinners around these loss leaders, you can save big dough.

- **Unit prices.** Some items are sold in different-sized packages. Unless your supermarket lists the unit price on the shelf, you'll have to do the math yourself. You could bring a calculator or reach for your cell phone. Most wireless phones have a calculator function. For each item, divide the price by the number of units, such as ounces or pounds. That allows you to literally compare apples to apples.

If you go to the supermarket every week with a list of what you "need," you'll be paying far more than you have to. The idea is that when you "need" something, you should go to your own pantry or freezer and fetch the item, which you previously bought on sale.

QUICK TIP

Try supermarket store brands. They're so much better than the "generics" of a generation ago. In fact, many store brands are made by the same manufacturers that make name-brand food products.

How much can you save by stockpiling sale items? Most experts put the savings at around 20 percent of your entire food spending for a year. Considering the average American household of four spends about $7,000 on grocery food, housekeeping supplies, and personal-care items, you're talking about savings of about $1,400 a year. And that excludes other categories of supermarket items that go on sale, such as over-the-counter medications.

That's $1,400 in savings for buying the exact same items, but buying them at ideal times.

There can be drawbacks to this strategy. Obviously, perishables don't stockpile well. Don't buy more perishable food than you will reasonably use before it goes bad, or your savings will be lost. Also, some people, especially those living in urban areas, have less pantry and freezer space to stockpile supermarket items. The stockpiling system will only work on a smaller scale for those people.

Freezing Times

Freezer Storage Chart (0 °F)
Note: Freezer storage is for quality only.
Frozen foods remain safe indefinitely.

Item	Months
Bacon and sausage	1 to 2
Casseroles	2 to 3
Egg whites or egg substitutes	12
Frozen dinners and entrees	3 to 4
Gravy, meat, or poultry	2 to 3
Ham, hot dogs, and lunch meats	1 to 2
Meat, uncooked roasts	4 to 12
Meat, uncooked steaks or chops	4 to 12
Meat, uncooked ground	3 to 4
Meat, cooked	2 to 3
Poultry, uncooked whole	12
Poultry, uncooked parts	9
Poultry, uncooked giblets	3 to 4
Poultry, cooked	4
Soups and stews	2 to 3
Wild game, uncooked	8 to 12

Source: USDA

For more information on freezing food, go online to www.fsis.usda.gov/FactSheets/Focus_ On_ Freezing/index.asp

Cherry-Picking Pays

Consumers who regularly visit multiple supermarkets and "cherry-pick" the best deals not only save money, but also save enough to offset the time it takes to do the extra shopping. This is the conclusion of an academic study by University of Pennsylvania Wharton marketing professor Stephen J. Hoch and Edward J. Fox, a marketing professor at the Cox School of Business at Southern Methodist University.

How is this possible? First, these supershoppers' advance preparation allows them to get significant price reductions on a number of items. Second, and more important, they compound those savings by purchasing multiple items when they're cheap. Savings from visiting a second store alone paid the equivalent of about $16 per hour. Considering price inflation since the study was conducted, that's nearing $20 per hour today.

QUICK TIP

Warehouse clubs, such as Costco, Sam's Club, and BJ's Wholesale, are great for some items and not for others. They can end up saving more than the membership fee if you're judicious about what you buy. For example, paper goods are often cheaper at a warehouse club. Your price list will advise you on what the best deals are. Of course, you don't want to buy perishable food in such large quantities that you end up throwing out a large portion that spoils.

3. Match Coupons to Sales

You can save significant money by doing the first two steps and skipping coupons. But you certainly will be leaving money on the table.

For the most savings, you'll want to match a coupon with a sale. This is the big secret for the most strategic of shoppers. For those shoppers, about two-thirds of their savings comes from shopping sales. An additional one-third comes from using coupons.

However, the key with coupons is to avoid hassle. If you have the time and inclination to clip coupons, neatly file them in some type of organizer and weed out expired coupons, go for it. Many people have their own filing systems or use such products as the Couponizer, found at www.couponizer.com.

One low-hassle way is the CouponMom system. Get the coupon circulars from the Sunday newspaper, write the date on the front and put them aside, perhaps in a closet or drawer. In preparing to go shopping, go online to CouponMom.com. It is free, although you must register.

CouponMom has two main tools. The first is "Grocery Deals by State," which each week lists the best deals at your local supermarket, noting sales and coupons. For coupons, it will tell you the date and the circular to clip the coupon from. That way, you can fetch the coupon circulars from the closet or drawer and clip coupons only as you're going to use them.

The Web site also has a listing of all current coupons in its "Grocery Coupon Database." If your supermarket isn't listed in "Grocery Deals by State," you can choose sale items you want in the weekly circular and look them up in the database to determine whether there's a matching coupon.

A similar system is at TheGroceryGame.com. It has a small fee, but has a free trial. Some users like it better, especially because it includes unadvertised sales and firmly advises you on what's a good deal versus a great deal. HotCouponWorld.com is another good site, mostly for hard-core strategic shoppers. It has a robust message forum where frugal denizens trade shopping tips. It is free.

---

302 billion—Number of coupons offered in 2007

2.6 billion—Number of coupons redeemed in 2007

$150,000+—Household income for biggest users of coupons

80%—Portion of coupon users who are female
Source: 2007 CMS Consumer Study

FIGURE 3.1   *Coupons: by the numbers*

If you're looking for low hassle, just use Sunday newspaper coupons. If you're more enthusiastic, you'll want online printable coupons too. Besides some of the Web sites already mentioned, get online coupons from such sites as SmartSource.com, Coupons.com, CoolSavings.com, and Eversave.com. There are literally dozens of other sites you can find with an Internet search engine, but after viewing a few, you'll discover they offer mostly the same coupons.

QUICK TIP

Pay attention to "Catalinas." These are checkout coupons handed to shoppers with grocery store receipts. The coupons, named after Catalina Marketing—the company that pioneered their use— often lead to savings and free items.

The big-picture strategy here is to recognize a good price on supermarket items. When you find one, you pounce, by stockpiling and slapping a coupon on it.

Fun Tangent: Razor Blades

Razor blades are among those repeat purchases at the supermarket or drug store that can tick off consumers more than many others. That's because replacement cartridges on higher-end shavers can be so expensive.

To save money, you could buy cheaper blades, but many consumers claim the more expensive new razors with more blades are, indeed, superior. So, the other way to spend less is to make blades last longer.

How? Dry your razor blades daily.

Razor blade dullness occurs more from oxidation—rusting—than from contact with whiskers. Water resting on blades between shaves causes the rusting. So keep your razors dry. After every use, shake it vigorously to dislodge water droplets, blot it on a towel and even give it a brief blow-drying if a hairdryer is nearby. It's also a good idea to store your razor outside the bathroom to avoid steam and humidity from getting to blades. Or store the dry razor in a sealable plastic bag.

My own test involved drying a Gillette Fusion razor after every use. I used the same cartridge for three months, compared with the usual two weeks. And I've been drying my razors ever since.

Food Away from Home

The first rule of dining out for less is to do it infrequently. By all means, go out to celebrate a wedding anniversary or job promotion. But try to avoid loading the family in the car and going to a restaurant because you're a poor meal planner. And when dining out, look for reasonable ways to cut your tab without cutting enjoyment.

Food Away from Home, 1-2-3

1. **Make freezer meals.**
2. **Use coupons and discounts.**
3. **Skimp on what you don't care about.**

1. Make Freezer Meals

We've all done it. Dinnertime sneaks up on us, we don't have anything planned and don't feel like cooking. The easiest solution is takeout, delivery, or schlepping to the nearest chain restaurant.

The simple solution is freezer meals. It's different from simple leftovers in the fridge. With freezer meals, you make double and triple batches when you cook—hamburgers, meatloaf, casserole, whatever. Then on those harried evenings, you're only microwave minutes away from a quicker, more healthful, and less-expensive entrée than you probably would get dining out. Whip up a few quick sides, and presto! A meal.

A little meal planning goes a long way toward saving money—and not just on dinner. Taking lunch to work instead of buying is, admittedly, obvious and tired advice. But do you brown-bag it every day? Ask yourself why not. And what about that morning latte from Starbucks that every money advice-giver wants to cut from your morning routine? Well, that's up to you, of course. Just make sure it's truly how you want to spend your money. You might have seen the math before, but I'll repeat it here: Cut a $4 coffee and $7 lunch each workday, and you save $2,750 a year. If nearly three grand is no big deal to you and you don't need to spend it on something else, then eat out.

2. Use Coupons and Discounts

Granted, if a man is on a first date, he might not want to whip out coupons when the bill comes, unless he knows his date is of like-minded frugality. But coupons and discounts can save significant money on dining out.

One secret method keeps anyone from knowing you're getting a discount. Sign up at RewardsNetwork.com. Tell them what credit cards and debit cards you use to pay for meals, and if you dine at a participating restaurant, you get a discount automatically credited to your credit or debit account. You do nothing—no coupons or gift certificates. Discounts are typically 5 percent to 10 percent.

Also check out Restaurant.com, OpenTable.com, and the ubiquitous Entertainment book from Entertainment.com. If you're looking for a cheap way to take the kids out, look for special deals at KidsMealDeals.com.

3. Skimp on What You Don't Care About

Sometimes, we're on autopilot at a restaurant, ordering a soft drink, appetizer, entrée, and dessert. Then we wonder why we're so uncomfortably full when we leave. Cut out what you don't care about.

Do you like free water just as well as a $3 soft drink? Can you wait until you get home for a beer or glass of wine? Can you skip the appetizer or eat an appetizer and skip the entrée? Are the portions big enough to share an entrée? What about skipping the tempting dessert and coming back some other time for dessert only?

This isn't rocket science, but it does take discipline and a willingness to break your routine. Listen to your body about how hungry you actually are and order less. And look for reasonable substitutions that will cut your tab without cutting your enjoyment.

Insurance

Insurance is a wide-ranging topic, and some people have unique insurance needs. But here are three things almost everybody can do to save money.

Insurance, 1-2-3

1. **Say no to extended warranties and other junk insurance.**
2. **Refinance your term life insurance.**
3. **Raise deductibles on home and auto insurance.**

1. Say No to Extended Warranties and Other Junk Insurance

Keep things simple and don't outsmart yourself. There's a lot of junk insurance out there that is way too expensive for the risk it covers.

Extended warranties are at the top of the list. Just don't buy them. How's that for simple? Don't buy them on electronics, computers, cars, appliances, or anything else. Does anybody really think a $40 extended warranty on a $200 camera is a good deal?

Are there examples of extended warranties paying off? Of course. And there are examples at a casino roulette wheel, when the ball falls into the number 8 slot. There's also a chance you might die from a snake bite this year. It's just not very likely. The point is, almost all extended warranties are a lousy bet.

Similarly, don't sign up for a home warranty, or service contract, which is essentially insurance on your appliances and major operating systems, like a furnace.

You can skip many of these insurances if you maintain an emergency fund to pay for repairs. Here's a simple concept: When stuff breaks, pay to repair it. Don't make it more complicated than that. You'll save money in the end.

Here's an idea—self insure. Whenever you're tempted to buy an extended warranty, say no. Then put the money you would have spent on the warranty into a separate bank account. That will act as your repair fund. Chances are that over time, you'll put far more into the account than you spend on repairs.

I'm not necessarily saying you should check your brain at the door and blindly reject every offer. But you'll do well to make "no" your default answer and set a high hurdle for saying "yes."

2. Refinance Your Term Life Insurance

Term life insurance premiums have been plummeting for years. So, if you have an old policy, it's time to get a new one, and then cancel the old one. In all likelihood, you can either save a lot of money or get a lot more coverage for the same money, even though you're older than when you first took out the policy.

I call this "refinancing" because it's so similar to refinancing your house mortgage to a better interest rate, only replacing your life insurance is better because the switch is free. It's a no-brainer.

You can save literally hundreds of dollars a year, which compounded over the life of a 15-year or 20-year policy amounts to thousands in savings.

What exactly is life insurance? A life insurance company pays your beneficiaries a lump sum of money if you die while the policy is in place.

A quick rule of thumb on whether you need life insurance: If anyone depends on your income, you need life insurance. So, single, childless people probably don't need it. An example of an exception is a stay-at-home mom. If a surviving working dad would have to hire childcare and other services the stay-at-home mom performed, you might want a small policy on her.

A quick rule of thumb on how much life insurance to buy: Get 6 to 10 times your income. This is a fuzzy number, like so much in financial planning is. So buy as close to 10 times your income as you can reasonably afford. Or, you can go through some laborious guestimate calculators online at Bankrate.com, Moneycentral.msn.com, Insurance.com, and AccuQuote.com. Be aware you're likely to get wildly different estimates.

How do you refinance your term life insurance? In short:

- Find a better price on guaranteed "level" term, which means coverage is guaranteed throughout the policy's term and the premium will not change.
- Sign up and take a physical.
- Cancel your old policy or let it lapse by not paying the premium.
- Save money.

Be sure to get your new policy in place *before* canceling your old policy. That way, if the medical examination discovers some disease or condition that makes you uninsurable, you can just keep the old policy.

Start by asking your existing life insurance company what current premiums would be for the same coverage. Then go online to life-insurance comparison sites, such as AccuQuote.com, SelectQuote.com, Insure.com, Efinancial.com and Intelliquote.com. Be aware that some sites will give you an instant quote on life insurance, while others simply pass your name on to insurance brokers who will contact you. The sites listed previously should give you an instant quote.

If you're having trouble deciding on a site, use AccuQuote.com, one of the oldest comparison sites on the Web. It also offers help by telephone, 1-800-442-9899. You get the same rate regardless of whether you get a quote online or with help on the phone.

How do you know if the quote you received is from a good insurance company? Only consider companies rated A-plus or above. Many comparison sites list the ratings along with the price quotes, or you could check them out yourself at such rating sites as standardandpoors.com, ambest.com and fitchratings.com.

QUICK TIP

Don't buy child life insurance or specific-death insurance. You don't depend on a child's income, so don't buy life insurance for a kid. And if you need life insurance, it doesn't matter how you die—cancer, heart attack, or stepping off the curb and getting hit by the proverbial bus. So don't buy specific-death insurance. Just get regular term insurance.

Don't have term life insurance? Do you have whole life, universal life, variable life, or some other cockamamie cash-value life insurance policy with an investment component? You might do better to cash it in and get regular term insurance. It will be far cheaper. Or looked at another way, you could be getting a lot more life insurance for the same money. The problem is that permanent life insurance policies are so complicated, they're difficult to analyze. To help decide whether to dump a cash-value policy, get an analysis of your policy for a relatively small fee at the Consumer Federation of America, at EvaluateLifeInsurance.org. An expert there, James Hunt, a former insurance commissioner of Vermont, will analyze your policy for a reasonable fee, which at this writing was $70 or $80, depending on the type of policy. He'll recommend what you should do with your policy.

Contact information: James H. Hunt, 8 Tahanto St., Concord, NH 03301-3835, jameshhunt@cs.com, 603-224-2805. Okay to call on evenings and weekends.

3. Raise Deductibles on
Home and Auto Insurance

Insurance is to protect you from financial disaster, not minor money annoyances. That's partly why you want high deductibles on your home and auto insurance. Another reason is answered with a question: What do you think will happen if you submit an auto insurance claim for a few hundred dollars? That's right. You insurer might fire you as a customer and cancel your insurance. So, if you're not going to make small claims—and you shouldn't—you might as well raise your deductibles. A deductible is the amount you have to pay before insurance starts paying. When you raise deductibles, the insurance company lowers the premium you have to pay.

Consider deductibles of $500 or even $1,000 on auto insurance, and $1,000 to $2,500 on home insurance. You'll save 15 percent to 30 percent off your premiums.

QUICK TIP

Insurance for home and especially auto can vary dramatically from insurer to insurer. It pays to periodically shop around. Yes, it's a pain. But, yes, it's worth it. Today, you can get quotes online at such sites as www.insurance.com, www.instantquote.com, or www.insweb.com.

Telecommunications

I'm going to lump several types of services together under telecommunications because more and more, that's how consumers buy them. I'm talking about services for your home phone, wireless phone, pay television, and Internet access.

The big idea with telecommunications is to pay attention. These services are evolving so quickly that new services and new prices are offered all the time. It pays to evaluate all your telecom services at least annually, if not quarterly. When it comes to telecom, paying attention pays off.

Telecommunications, 1-2-3

1. **Cancel your traditional landline phone service.**
2. **Rightsize your wireless phone plan.**
3. **Regularly review TV and Internet service.**

1. Cancel Your Traditional Landline Phone Service

"No way! He did *not* just suggest dumping my house phone line."

Oh, yes, he did.

A dial tone to your home phone has become a commodity. That means it's not special anymore. And it's definitely not worth paying $40 a month for service, plus extra for long-distance calls. Today, unlimited, free long-distance calls are a throw-in feature, like call-waiting or caller ID.

You can get phone service so many ways nowadays that traditional landline phone service from a Ma Bell descendent has become a dinosaur. That's why you should consider dumping your traditional stand-alone landline altogether. Here are a few ideas:

- **Subscribe to a bundle.** Phone and cable companies are fighting over customers for their triple-play services—TV, Internet, and phone. Landline phone service has become such a commodity that it's not even the highlight of the triple play. Bundled phone service often includes unlimited long-distance calls and a wide host of features, such as voice mail, call-waiting, and caller ID. If you already subscribe to pay TV and Internet access, you might save money by moving all your services under one roof and buying a bundle.

- **Use wireless only.** The ability to place and receive phone calls is no longer necessarily tied to the copper phone wires running throughout your home. That's a mental hurdle to overcome, for sure.

  But more people are dumping landline service and using only a wireless phone as they get used to calling people, not places. A generation ago, callers would dial up a place, such as a home or an office because phones were literally tied to buildings. Today, wireless phones are associated with individuals, so people call other people, not buildings. As wireless phones become commonplace, it's harder to justify duplicate landline telephone service.

Before cutting the cord, make sure you have adequate reception throughout your home. New technologies are evolving. Some allow you to put a small base station in your home to boost wireless signals by some carriers. If you currently get poor reception, keep an eye out for these new technologies, one of which is called *femtocell*. This refers to adding a small base station in your house that uses your broadband Internet connection to boost your cell-phone signal and improve call quality.

The second caveat is to have enough minutes on your wireless plan to handle calls at home and on the go.

- **Consider Voice over Internet Protocol (VOIP).** Consumers have many choices for using their broadband Internet connection as a phone line, using VOIP. Skype and Vonage are examples of Internet-based phone services. Several traditional phone companies also offer VOIP service. It can be far less expensive than a traditional stand-alone phone line. And if you have strong, reliable broadband Internet service, call quality can be quite good.

The MagicJack Phone Solution

MagicJack, www.MagicJack.com, offers phone service with unlimited long distance, voice mail, caller ID, call-waiting, and other features for $20 per year. That's per year.

For an additional $20, you must buy a small, matchbox-sized device that plugs into the flat USB port on your computer. You plug a phone line and phone into the other end of the device. Software loads onto your computer automatically and you get a dial tone. So, to get started, the device plus a year's service costs about $40, and you never get a monthly bill.

You can use MagicJack as a landline by plugging a cordless phone system base into the MagicJack line and adding multiple handsets throughout the house.

Drawbacks of MagicJack include not being able to keep your existing phone number. You'll get a new one. And you must have the computer on to place and receive calls. If it's off, incoming calls go to voicemail. The company is working on solutions to both of those disadvantages, MagicJack inventor Dan Borislow tells me.

And although MagicJack works flawlessly for many people, including myself, others seem to have problems. The service is only as good as your broadband Internet connection. Voice quality can range from as good as a landline to as poor as a cell phone with a weak signal. Use several online speed tests to measure your connection speed. Find tests by entering into your favorite search engine "VOIP speed test."

Use the 30-day money-back guarantee to try MagicJack before canceling landline service to make sure it works for you.

2. Rightsize Your Wireless Phone Plan

I'm not going to tell you exactly what wireless plan to get. For one thing, offerings seem to change almost monthly. Second, people's needs differ depending on how they use the phone. Someone who uses the phone for hours a day and has substituted it for their landline phone needs a different plan than someone who has a cell phone for emergencies.

But I can tell you how you should decide for yourself.

The big idea in buying wireless service is not to pay for more service than you actually use. That might sound obvious. But consumers waste a tremendous amount of money on wireless phone plans. Largely, the waste comes in the form of paying for unused minutes, month after month, year after year.

Consumers on a monthly plan used an average of 461 calling minutes per month in 2008, according to J.D. Power and Associates. Considering most plans include far more minutes than that, many people are overpaying.

Here's my big point on cell phones: Literally millions of people on monthly contract plans would be far better off using pay-as-you-go prepaid cell phones. They can be the best choice now for light and even moderate users. That's especially true for those who use their phone mostly for talking, rather than advanced features such as texting and Internet access. How does prepaid work? Each company is a little different. But generally, you buy the phone. Some are very cheap, starting at $10 for the simplest phones. Then, you buy minutes to load onto the phone. You can buy minutes online or in stores, in the form of a card with a code that you enter into the phone. Some of the better deals come from prepaid providers ranking high on a recent J.D. Power customer satisfaction survey. See Figure 3.2.

Here are the three national providers of prepaid service that rank above the industry average:

- Tracfone (and sister company Net10)
- Virgin Mobile
- T-Mobile To Go

Source: J.D. Power and Associates 2008 Prepaid Customer Satisfaction Survey

Note: Cricket and MetroPCS also ranked above average, but they don't have nationwide coverage.

FIGURE 3.2   *Above-average prepaid providers*

Here's a rule of thumb based on prices in 2008: If you typically use fewer than 400 minutes each month, prepaids are worth a look. Check your recent bills for how many minutes you actually use. Many people could cut their total cell service expense to about $10 per month or less, all fees and taxes included. And prepaid plans are getting so much better so quickly that as of early 2009, *Consumer Reports* magazine says even heavy cell-phone users might be able to save money with a prepaid phone.

You can retain your current cell phone number by "porting" it to the prepaid carrier. And call quality is generally good because prepaids use the same wireless networks as the traditional wireless carriers. Of course, like with the big contract carriers, call quality varies by region and even community.

Should you switch to prepaid? The math to compare prepaid and monthly contract plans isn't that difficult. Look at recent bills to find the average minutes per month you actually use.

Divide your total monthly wireless bill, taxes and fees included, by your average minutes. This is your true cost per minute. Compare that to the cost per minute of a prepaid plan. One of the easiest prepaid plans to compare is Net10, found at www.net10.com. It's 10 cents per minute, period. Taxes and fees are already included in the price of prepaid minutes.

So, a traditional $39.99 monthly plan that costs about $48 after taxes and fees and includes 450 minutes would have a per-minute cost of about 11 cents, which is close to the Net10 prepaid price. However, that assumes you use all 450 minutes every month. If you use only 125 minutes and lose the rest, your cost soars to 38 cents per minute, which is a lousy rate.

Other advantages of prepaids are you have no contracts, no early-termination fees, and no credit checks.

Of course, there are downsides. Prepaids tend to offer older name-brand phones, which might not have the most current features. And prepaid rules can be confusing until you learn them. For example, prepaid minutes expire. The more minutes you buy, the longer they last, typically up to a year.

QUICK TIP

If you'll be sticking with prepaid for a while, add min-utes that will last a year, so you don't have to worry about when they'll expire.

Most prepaid services offer nationwide access, but some charge for roaming outside a home region. A few carriers charge an access fee of $1, for example, on days you use the phone. But they might offer free calls to other wireless users on the same network for unlimited calls on nights and weekends.

Again, that complexity is why a simplified system like Net10 is attractive.

If you're uncertain, you can test-drive a pay-as-you-go prepaid phone. Go to a store or online and buy a prepaid phone that has some starter minutes on it. Test the call quality in your home and around your region. If you don't like it, you lose little. You spent $10 or $20 to potentially save hundreds a year.

My Prepaid Phone Story

For years, my wife and I had one of those "fam-ily plans" from a well-known phone company. We use our phones frequently, several times a week, but we don't talk for many minutes. We were using an average of just 150 minutes per month but paying for 700 minutes, the least you could get with a family plan.

I switched both of us to prepaid cell phones. Savings per year: $800.

Bonus benefit: Call quality in my home is actually better with the prepaid than with the pricier monthly contract plan. Go figure.

So, if prepaids are such a good deal, why aren't more Americans using them? Why are people making an illogical choice to pay more?

Apparently, there is widespread uncertainty and some damaging misconceptions that keep people loyal to their contract plans, says a study in late 2008 by the New Millennium Research Council.

Foremost among these myths is that more than half of people think they are always under contract with their wireless carrier and always must pay a fee to switch, according to the survey. Of course, you might have to pay a fee, especially if you continue to upgrade your handset and accept two-year commitment renewals of your contract. But more wireless carriers are prorating the early-termination fee, which reduces the fee to get out of your contract. Many others are on month-to-month with no commitment, but they don't know it.

See Figure 3.3 for other myths about prepaid phones.

- Nearly 6 out of 10 Americans (59 percent) including 70 percent of 18–24 year olds—mistakenly believe that prepaid phones "are good only for people who rarely, if ever, use their cell phones." Less than one-third (32 percent) of respondents knew that this is a myth.

- More Americans than not mistakenly believe that prepaid phones are only available in "very basic models."

- Americans split evenly on whether this myth was accurate: "Prepaid cell phone plans where you pay for the minutes you use always cost *more* per month than contract-based cell phone plans where you pay a monthly fee."

- Only half know that it is untrue that "prepaid phones don't get very good reception and only work in certain places."

- Less than half know that it is untrue that "you can't get voice mail, text, or take photos on a prepaid phone."

Source: "Prepaid Phones in the U.S.: Myths, Lack of Consumer Knowledge Blocking Wider Use," prepared for the New Millennium Research Council by Opinion Research Corp.

FIGURE 3.3   *Prepaid phone myths*

Of course, pay-as-you-go prepaids are not for everybody. Here are your other basic choices:

- **No wireless.** Yes, this *is* an option. Today, half of Americans consider a cell phone one of their untouchable "necessity" expenses they can't live without, according to a 2006 study by the Pew Research Center. A decade earlier, cell phones didn't even make the list.

If you truly "need" a cell phone for emergencies, you can use any charged cell phone to dial 911, even if it has no service plan. Ask around to family and friends. Somebody will give you an old phone for free. Any household typically has several lying in a drawer somewhere.

And if you have a cell phone for work and your company doesn't care whether you make personal calls with it—perhaps the work phone is on an unlimited-minutes plan—it doesn't make much sense to get your own phone too.

- **Regular monthly contract.** If you use a lot of minutes each month, for example, 500 or more, a traditional plan might be the way to go. It's also best if you do a lot of texting and Internet access on the phone. Or, if you must have the latest feature-rich phones, like the iPhone by Apple that was so hot, you'll need a monthly plan.

  Again, this is where you must assess what you will really use. It might be cool to look up a stock quote, sports score, or news story on your phone. But if you're the type who will try out such services and never return to them, paying for such features month after month will amount to a lot of wasted money. Know yourself.

- **Unlimited plan.** Relatively new, unlimited plans let you talk as much as you want. They came out at $100 per month, which was about the price for 2,000 minutes per month. Think about that. The allure of "unlimited" is that 33 hours a month on the phone is simply not enough time?

But if you really talk that much, an unlimited plan might be for you. Just be clear about what it includes. Is that unlimited talking? Or unlimited texting and data too?

Online comparison tools for choosing wireless plans are fine to use. They might provide ideas about which plans might be right for you. But, through 2008, I'm not overly impressed with how good a job they do recommending the right plan to fit each individual's needs. Some to try include MyRatePlan.com, Wirefly.com, and LetsTalk.com. One other, BillShrink.com, is very slick and has a lot of potential because it recommends the very best plan for you, based on your actual use. It even explains why it chose the plan based on your needs. It's worth checking out.

Note that I didn't dwell on buying the phone itself. First, your purchase decision on wireless should be made based on the price and quality of service, not the hardware. That's because you'll spend far more on service, no matter what pricey phone you buy. Second, a phone is a one-time purchase. It's over and done with. It's a relatively small amount of money. However, a wireless contract goes on and on, month after month, costing big money in the long run. Information on phones themselves can be found at such Web sites as Cnet.com, PhoneScoop.com, ConsumerReports.org, and ConsumerSearch.com.

3. Regularly Review TV and Internet Service

Like phone service, pay TV and Internet service continue to evolve. That's good because consumers will have more choices. And robust competition could drive down prices. But it's bad because the sheer number of choices makes choosing a service more confusing—a lot more confusing. Nowadays, many consumers can get phone service from their cable TV company and pay television service from their phone company.

If you must have pay TV and Internet service—and unless you're living in poverty or are deeply in debt, it's not unreasonable—the easiest move is to buy them as part of a bundle from your cable or phone service provider. The drawback is that although you might get discounts compared with buying the same services separately, you'll probably get services you don't really need or want, especially TV channels you will never watch. However, to get services better tailored to your needs, you would have to become an expert on each service and try to cobble together services a la carte.

The point here, whether you buy services in a bundle or not, is to regularly review them and keep an eye out for new offers that might fit your life better. Offerings and prices are changing all the time.

Television

The following are your basic choices for television service, some you've heard of and perhaps a few you haven't:

- **Broadcast only.** This option has become a much better option lately. That's because with a set-top antenna, many people can pull in high-definition broadcast television signals to display on their newer HDTVs.

  The best part? It's absolutely free.

Your picture will be even better than that of pay-TV customers who get high-definition signals from cable, satellite, or fiber-optic. That's because signals snatched out of the air are less compressed. People who live farther away from transmitting stations might need a more powerful rooftop antenna to receive signals.

In many areas, you can get digital broadcasts from the major networks, including ABC, CBS, NBC, FOX, CW, and PBS. As long as you have an HDTV, the picture will be far superior to any analog signal you've ever seen. However, those who live in remote areas, in valleys, or in urban areas with many tall buildings nearby might receive a limited selection of stations or none at all, leaving pay TV as the only option.

Of course, the big drawback of going with antenna-only is you won't get such cable channels as HBO, ESPN, CNN, The Food Network, and many others. You'll need subscription TV to receive them. That might be a deal breaker for using an antenna only. As a hybrid move, you can subscribe to a basic tier of pay TV service to get cable channels and use your antenna to receive digital and high-def broadcast networks—forgoing high-def versions of cable channels. You'll save the cost of upgrading to the digital tier to get HD programming.

If you have an older non-HD television, you can still get reception with an antenna. But you will need a converter box for each TV. The government has been issuing coupons worth $40 to help defray the cost of converter boxes, which cost about $50. Learn more at www.DTV2009.gov online or call 1-888-388-2009.

QUICK TIP

There's no such thing as an HDTV antenna. An antenna is an antenna. Slapping an HDTV label on the box is just marketing. It's actually easier to pick up new digital signals than old analog signals. You shouldn't get the old "ghosts" or "snow" with digital signals. It's either perfect or unwatchably pixilated. To choose an appropriate antenna, go online to antennaweb.org. It will help you select one.

- **Pay television.** Of course, you can pay for TV through a cable or satellite company. And, increasingly, phone companies are starting to offer pay television as they roll out fiber-optic networks.

- **QAM tuner with cable.** Here's a secret not many people know: You can get free HDTV with the most basic cable TV package and no cable box. It's a little techie, but it might save you money.

  You'll need a high-definition television with a Quadrature Amplitude Modulation (QAM) tuner. Newer TVs have QAM tuners, and your TV's instruction manual should specify if it does. Alternatively, you could buy a stand-alone QAM tuner. You'll also need a cable TV package, even if it's the cheapest broadcast-only package.

  Screw the coaxial cable wire directly into your TV. Then, go into your HDTV setup menu. For the source of the signal, select something like "digital cable" or DTV. The exact term varies by TV manufacturer. Then force your TV to automatically search for channels. When it's done, scroll through the channels.

With digital channels, you'll find multiple subchannels under the same number, labeled something like 87-2. The digital channels should look noticeably better. And when a digital program is broadcast in high-definition, it will fill the elongated screen of your HDTV and look fantastic.

The channels will have weird-looking names with lots of numbers in them, but your TV should allow you to change the on-screen label to ABC, CBS, CW, and so on.

How is this useful? If you use your HDTV in the bedroom or den for limited TV watching and you don't want to pay for another HD cable box, you can use this method to get broadcast digital and HD channels for no additional cost. Or, if you only need the broadcast channels, you can drop to the lowest level of nondigital cable TV service and still get digital and HD broadcasts.

Again, you will mostly get broadcast channels, meaning no ESPN or Discovery Channel. Those channels are encrypted and not accessible with the QAM tuner. You also won't get an interactive TV schedule grid, and you won't be able to pull up "on-demand" content. Your QAM tuner doesn't work with satellite TV signals.

• **Online.** More and more television content is available online to those with high-speed Internet connections. For example, many broadcast networks offer full-length shows at their Web sites for free.

You can buy shows from Apple's iTunes music store and Amazon.com Video on Demand. Shows and movies are free at aggregation sites, such as Hulu.com, Joost.com, and even YouTube.com. Older movies, too, are often available online for free.

I don't watch a lot of television, but my wife and I often watch a show or two before bedtime. During the television writers' strike in late 2007 and early 2008, there was nothing new on TV. So, at the nearby video store, we rented DVDs of the television cop series, *The Shield* (which is a great show but probably too violent and rough for some tastes). Anyway, we watched all the seasons of *The Shield* that the video store had, which excluded the most recent one. So, we downloaded that season from iTunes to a laptop computer. We hooked the computer to a TV, and were able to enjoy the missing season. Another time, we were watching a recorded episode of *The Unit* when the ending was cut off because the show's start had been delayed by a football game. We fired up the computer and watched the last five minutes on CBS.com.

Of course, most people want to watch shows on a large television screen, not a small computer screen. The easiest method to do that is to hook a laptop computer to a television with a set of cables. Which type of cables you need depends on the outputs from your computer and the inputs to your TV. I've found personnel at stores like RadioShack can be helpful in getting what I need in those situations, although the price of the cables might not be the lowest.

Standalone devices can help you watch online content on your television. Examples are a Roku player, Tivo and such game consoles as the Xbox 360 and Playstation 3. Among the big drawbacks of "going off the grid" with TV is the relative dearth of free live sports programming available online. Most streamed sports games are available by subscription only or are illegal to access.

Internet TV might not have all the content you want, but it could be a supplement. It might allow you to cancel cable and go with free antenna reception or drop to a lower tier of pay-TV service.

Fun Tangent:
Don't Overpay for Audio-Video Cables

One of the biggest rip-offs in electronics retailing is overpriced cables. These cables travel various routes, to and from the TV, cable or satellite box, receiver, DVD player, and speakers.

Here's a good rule: Go for digital over analog when deciding among types of cables. But among brands of cables, feel free to cheap out. That could mean buying a $5 HDMI cable—the best connection for a high-definition TV—instead of a $100 HDMI cable.

Why? Because there's no difference in the quality of sound and picture you get from pricey cables. It's true that high-priced cables are high quality, made of good materials with good connections, and they look nice too. They're probably even more durable. But, as counterintuitive as it sounds, top-quality cables won't make your TV's picture or sound any better than cheap cables of the same type and gauge.

Don Lindich, a syndicated technology columnist and creator of SoundAdviceBlog.com, puts it this way: Buying expensive cables is like using Evian bottled water to flush your toilet. It might be top-quality purified water, but it doesn't flush the bowl any better than tap water.

For example, if you have a newer HDTV and cable box that can use an HDMI connection, use it. It's higher quality than other connections. But don't spend $75 or $100 on a cord. Discounters, such as Wal-Mart and Target, often sell reasonably priced cables. Perhaps the best combination of price and quality is available at online retailers, such as Monoprice.com, where I got a 6-foot HDMI cable for $5.24 plus shipping. It works great. Amazon.com too often has high-quality but inexpensive HDMI cables.

The same goes for wires to speakers. For runs of 50 feet or less, 16-gauge electrical wire—even if it's lamp cord—is all you need. Gauge matters. Brand does not. However, you can't totally cheap out on cables and speaker wire running inside of walls. In many areas, building codes require the wire to be rated for "in-wall use," a feature easily found on packaging or retail displays.

Internet Access

You'll notice many of the suggestions in this book are tightly tied with looking up information on the Internet. So having at least a slow-speed dial-up connection is a good idea. Of course, you could use free Internet access at a library or wireless Internet access at public "wi-fi hot spots," such as a coffee shop.

However, having Internet access at home is convenient. Internet service can help with skillful shopping, which will save far more money than access will cost.

You'll need to evaluate what Internet service providers (ISPs) are available to you. Generally, it will be through your phone line or cable line, although plans to roll out wide area wireless networks are in the early stages. Internet access via cell-phone networks is also becoming more common. You can get Internet access via satellite, but that's traditionally been an expensive option, making sense only for those without other choices, such as people living in very rural regions.

Availability of these Internet-access options varies among communities. If you're uncertain which to choose, seek advice from a tech-oriented friend or relative who lives nearby.

This is one area I would not skimp on. Get the fastest Internet service you can reasonably afford.

So, again, the big-picture idea with telecommunications is to stay informed about the new offerings and prices. That way, you can rightsize your spending for what you actually use.

Chapter 4

How to Buy Stuff

"How to buy stuff?" you might be asking yourself when you read the title of this chapter. "Believe me, I don't need advice on how to buy stuff. I'm great at that. I need to know how *not* to buy stuff!"

But the truth is this: Buying things well is difficult if you don't have specific routines and some practice at doing it right. You'll regularly be buying thousands of dollars worth of goods and services for your entire life. You'll have needs, such as tires for your car, a plumber for a leaky faucet, and new eyeglasses. You'll have wants, such as a new television set, a second fabulous pair of black shoes, and a Caribbean vacation.

The point is to spend your money smarter on all of those things.

That segues into a discussion of needs and wants. It's so easy to confuse the two things. But learning the difference is "how *not* to buy stuff."

We *need* basic food, basic clothing, basic shelter, and basic transportation. Upgrades to those things are wants. Wants come in the form of dining out, name-brand clothing, a 3,000-square-foot house, and a sporty new sedan. All your entertainment spending is a want. Wants include vacations, video games, music CDs, cable television, and every piece of jewelry you own.

I'm not saying you should only spend money on necessities and deprive yourself of wants. I'm just saying you must be very clear in your mind about the difference. Then each purchase you make starts with an evaluation of the need and is upgraded with wants.

This reminds me of a business term, *zero-based budgeting*. The problem with typical budgeting is that the amount budgeted for future spending is strictly based on how much you spent in the past. The only debate is about whether your department's budget gets 3 percent more or 5 percent more. It's incremental budgeting. There's no examination of what you actually need, only how much more you'll spend in the future. After a few years, how much you're spending can be completely divorced from what you need to spend.

Meanwhile, zero-based budgeting is starting from scratch, or zero. All spending—the category of spending and the amount—has to be entirely rejustified. It's about building up your expenses from zero, rather than cutting down expenses from current levels. Or, as we've talked about, it's about whether a purchase is truly needed or we're just buying because that's what we always do.

That's a long way of saying that it's important to stay grounded. Make conscious decisions about whether you can get by with a functional brand or whether it's worthwhile to upgrade.

Some people say, "Well, I only buy the best for myself and my family. We deserve the best." Besides being silly and immature, that statement is illogical. Almost nobody outside of the likes of Bill Gates and Warren Buffet has enough money to have the best of everything. So we choose. Ideally, we choose by starting with needs and judiciously adding our wants.

One of the great by-products of spending your money smarter is that if you spend well on your needs, you'll have more money left for your wants.

Each section in this chapter gets straight to the point, with each starting with "How to..." In total, they are "How to buy stuff."

How to Buy Products

Is shopping around for products worth your time? You bet. And today it's easier than ever because of online reviews and price comparisons. Buying stuff breaks down into the three Rs: Read reviews, research prices, and reevaluate.

How to Buy Products, 1-2-3

1. **Read reviews**. Visit ConsumerReports.org, ConsumerSearch.com, and Amazon.com.
2. **Research prices**. See Froogle.com, MySimon.com, and Shopzilla.com.
3. **Reevaluate**. Wait a day before buying.

Granted, you don't need a three-step process for one-time purchases of less than $50, for example. But for bigger purchases or purchases you make repeatedly, it's well worth it.

A recent search for a Garmin Nuvi GPS navigator, like the one mentioned in the introduction of this book, turned up a variety of prices. The exact same model could cost anywhere from $345 to $900. That's a heck of a difference. How long did it take me to get that information? Less than 10 seconds on MySimon.com. Is 10 seconds of your time worth a $555 savings?

I'm not saying you should necessarily buy the least-expensive item for $345, especially if it's offered by an unfamiliar retailer with an amateurish Web site that doesn't pass the "smell" test for being legitimate. If one retailer is offering a price far below all the others, there might be something fishy. But after those well-invested 10 seconds, you'll have an excellent idea about the range of prices for that GPS system.

Armed with that knowledge, how likely are you now to visit a retail store and pay $900, knowing the average price is half that? Unlikely.

Granted, that was a fun example using a "want" item, a GPS navigator. But you can use this system on needs too.

1. Read Reviews

Some people are born researchers of products, while others are impulsive buyers of them. But if you'll be spending significant money, whatever you determine that to be, research can help you choose the right product.

The right product means one that fits your needs and is likely to be high quality. Nobody can be an expert on every purchase. You might know a lot about automobiles, but nothing about buying dishwashers. Perhaps you know a lot about cell phones, but nothing about buying a baby stroller.

Just as important, some quick research can reveal the range of possibilities within a product line—which features come with which model.

Just a generation ago, research was laborious. Maybe you visited several stores and talked to salespeople about the product. But if you need to buy a lawn mower, are you really going to visit a garden center and ask the salesperson which model you should buy? Salespeople can be very helpful, although it seems nowadays far less so. A salesperson has conflicting interests. He might have a genuine desire to do right by the customer. But a commissioned salesperson makes more money if he or she sells you a more expensive model of lawn mower, regardless of whether it's right for you.

So you need objective advice, or at least a variety of opinions, to make a smart spending choice.

Consulting a friend or relative is a good idea, as long as you realize that's just one person's experience and not the final word about the product. In the past, you could subscribe to *Consumer Reports* magazine, which has in-depth reviews. But you would have to wade through dozens of saved magazines trying to find the review you sought.

Because it was so difficult to find reviews, maybe you heavily researched purchases of homes, cars, and a few big-ticket items. And for the rest, you just winged it.

Today, because of the Internet, it's all different. You can research almost anything quickly.

For example, now, you can subscribe to *Consumer Reports'* online site and have instant access to reviews.

Rarely do I suggest spending money in order to save it. But an online subscription to *Consumer Reports*, found at www.consumerreports.org, is an exception. At the time of this writing, a subscription is a mere $26. That's a small price to pay for the outstanding product reviews and advice you receive. The advantage of the Web site over the magazine is the site is easily searchable. You can find the review you seek, even from years ago, in mere seconds.

The *Consumer Reports* site also offers blogs on such topics as cars, electronics, and products for babies and kids. Blogs are brief news items stacked chronologically, with the newest on top.

ConsumerSearch.com is another good resource. It's an aggregator of product reviews and gives a summary of what all the reviews seem to be saying. It's an efficient stop on the Web to get a lot of information quickly.

Mega online retailer Amazon.com is a good place to find reviews from actual users. Because Amazon.com sells a wide variety of products, it's worth a place in your Web browser's Favorites list, even if you never make a purchase from the retailer. Read a sampling of the good and bad reviews. But with user reviews, take comments with a grain of salt. Pay more attention to comments repeated in several reviews. Many retailers have user reviews on their Web sites now. So, if you were going to buy a particular model of LCD television, you might check large electronics retailer Best Buy to read reviews of the product on its site.

Another way to find reviews is to use your favorite search engine, such as Google.com. Type keywords that include the name and model of the product and the word "review." You'll likely find several reviews.

After a while, you'll find review sites that you like. For example, I like Cnet.com for reviews of electronics and software. Automobile reviews are available at such sites as Edmunds.com and Cars.com.

But if you want to keep it simple, check reviews at ConsumerReports.org, ConsumerSearch.com, and Amazon.com.

2. Research Prices

The point of price comparisons is to know what a good price is. Blindly accepting the first price you see is a conscious decision to be powerless as a consumer. In most cases, it's voluntarily paying more than you have to. And, come on, that's just plain dumb.

Again, we'll turn to the Internet to compare prices efficiently.

Among my favorite Web sites is Froogle.com, also known as Google Product Search. If you type a specific product into the main Google search window, a sampling of the product search results will appear on top. You can click through to view more. I also like MySimon.com and Shopzilla.com. These are all *shopbots*, like robots that go searching for prices on the Internet.

After visiting just a few shopbots, which literally could take about one minute, you'll have an excellent idea about the range of prices an item is being sold for. Be skeptical of prices that are far lower than others, especially if you click through to the retailer and the Web site looks amateurish. Included in some price comparisons will be refurbished products and listings on auction site eBay.com. So view those listings differently than new products from well-known retailers.

Speaking of eBay, that's also a prudent stop in your quest to find good prices. Many items are offered as new on eBay and are worth considering if you'll receive a deep discount in return for taking the risk of dealing with a person or merchant who might not be reputable. I've had good luck buying new items on eBay.

Just because you're searching online for prices doesn't mean you have to purchase online. You could still purchase in person locally. But knowing what a good price is before visiting a store arms you with information.

Opt for shopbots that include taxes and shipping charges. That way, you can get apples-to-apples comparisons on the total price of acquiring that product if you decide to buy it online.

You might find shopbots you like better, but good places to start are Froogle.com, MySimon.com, PriceGrabber.com, and Shopzilla.com.

> QUICK TIP
>
> *One promising service is Frucall. If you're standing at a store looking at an item and wondering whether it's being offered at a good price, you can find out. Pull out your cell phone and call 1-888-DO-FRUCALL and enter the product's barcode number. The automated service will recite several prices from online retailers. You can also get the information by text message or by going to a Web site. Find out more at Frucall.com.*

3. Reevaluate

We Americans generally aren't good at delayed gratification. But try to wait a day or more between wanting to make a purchase and actually making it. That delay gives you time to reflect on the needs versus wants issue I talked about earlier. Waiting helps mostly with optional purchases. But it also gives you time to reflect on a purchase you need but were thinking about upgrading, by buying a brand name or a product with more features.

> QUICK TIP
>
> *As a rule of thumb, wait one day for every $100 the purchase costs to avoid impulse buys. Of course, that rule works less well with very expensive items, such as a house or automobile. But for most purchases, it works well.*

I find that just the process of researching a product sometimes satisfies a buying impulse, or at least dampens it. Reading some negatives about the product, whether in professionally written reviews or user reviews, helps provide perspective that can also extinguish the buying desire.

Waiting allows that intense lust for acquiring something to subside. When you're clearheaded, you gain perspective about whether you really want it. Marketers know that time works against them. That's why high-pressure advertisements always tell you to "Buy now!" Infomercials entice you to buy, saying if you "buy now," you'll get bonus merchandise of some sort. It's why the car salesman says, "What do I have to do to get you in this new car *today*?"

There are very few purchasing opportunities that will disappear if you wait a day and reevaluate.

Quick Tip

If and when you go through with the purchase, you might be asked if you want to buy an extended warranty. Think about whether you want a warranty ahead of time, so you're prepared to answer the question. Almost all the time, the answer should be a flat-out, "No." See Chapter 3, "Get FIT (Food, Insurance, Telecommunications)," about insurance to learn why.

Price Protection

After you leave a store or check out of an online retailer, you're not quite done with your smart shopping. Even if you've done your due diligence on shopping for prices, a product might go on sale shortly after you purchased it. That infuriates shoppers.

That's why many retailers offer a price guarantee. Often it states that if the retailer lowers the price within 30 days after purchase—protection periods vary—it will refund you the difference. For example, if just before Christmas you bought a $1,500 television and its price in early January drops to $1,200, you could request a refund of $300.

In part, a store's price-protection guarantee is a sales tactic. It can give a buyer peace of mind and entice the shopper to buy immediately instead of looking elsewhere or delaying a purchase. It's regret insurance.

But really, price protection is a by-product of a retailer's return policy. If an item's price decreases, a diligent consumer who recently bought the item might return the old product and buy the sale-priced one, pocketing the difference. For the retailer, accepting the return and processing another sale involves hassle and expense. To avoid that, the retailer offers price protection, where it just refunds the money and skips the hassle of a return and resale.

However, few consumers are conscientious enough to review advertised prices after a purchase and then claim a price-protection refund. So, the retailer rarely has to make good on its price guarantee.

Therein lies the problem: It's up to you to watch prices *after* you buy.

But now, some free Web sites will watch for you, automatically notifying you when prices drop. That allows you to quickly and easily claim your refund. If you paid with a credit card, often the refund will be credited to your credit card account. Of course, price-protection policies vary from store to store.

If you bought a big-ticket item at a well-known retailer, you could monitor its weekly advertisements, often in the Sunday newspaper or online, for the duration of the price-protection period.

Easier, however, is to log purchases into a Web site, called PriceProtectr.com. PriceProtectr watches prices on literally dozens of retailers, such as Amazon.com, Best Buy, Circuit City, Gap, Costco, Sears, Staples, Macy's, Toys 'R Us, Home Depot, RadioShack, Target, and Wal-Mart.

The big idea is to log purchases into PriceProtectr, which will send an e-mail notifying you if the price decreases within the price-protection period. It's up to you to actually request the refund. Durations of price-protection guarantees vary widely by retailer—from 7 days to 90 days.

Obviously, this is a bit of a hassle. But at least try it for major purchases, of more than $500, for example. And log your purchases during major buying sprees—holiday-gift shopping or back-to-school shopping.

QUICK TIP

Yapta.com offers a price-protection service for airline flights you already booked.

How to Buy Services

Many purchases we make today aren't things, but services. We hire and subscribe all the time: home contractors and plumbers, mail-order movie services, gym memberships, airline flights, and hotel rooms.

How to Buy Services, 1-2-3

1. **Seek reviews and references.** Subscribe to Checkbook.org or Angieslist.com.
2. **Research prices by getting three price quotes.**
3. **Reevaluate and review contracts carefully.**

The three-step process for buying services is very similar to that for buying products. But you have a few different resources and tools available to you, along with some concerns that are specific to services.

If you look carefully, the steps are basically the same three Rs: Review, research prices, and reevaluate.

1. Seek Reviews and References

For products available nationwide, finding reviews is relatively easy. But where do you go for reviews of local service companies, such as plumbers, electricians, and photographers? If you are new to an area, you will need a slew of service providers, from a doctor and dentist to, perhaps, a dog kennel and dry cleaner.

Trial and error is an inefficient, and potentially expensive, way to find good service professionals. Talking with neighbors and local friends can work, but opinions come from a very small sample of customers, often one. Or you can obtain referrals from related professionals. For example, you could ask a lawyer to help find a good accountant.

Listings in the phone book and online can give you an idea of some of the providers available, as can advertisements in local media. But they don't give you objective advice on whom to choose and why.

Because choosing wisely means you might receive a better price and better service, here are some better resources:

- **Consumers' Checkbook.** www.checkbook.org is $30 or $34 for a one-year or two-year membership, depending on region. Membership in the nonprofit group Consumers' Checkbook, established in 1974, includes a semiannual magazine with articles and ratings, as well as access to its Web site, which has the most recent ratings of local service firms.

This is perhaps the most credible resource for unbiased reviews of local service companies. It accepts no advertising and has no business relationship with firms it rates.

Consumers' Checkbook doesn't just collect user reviews. It has a staff that does undercover price shopping, so it has apples-to-apples price comparisons, rather than asking members for their impressions about price. It also actively surveys consumers about the quality of service firms, rather than simply allowing anonymous posters to comment about firms, as some free Web sites do. Consumers' Checkbook won't officially list or evaluate a business until it has 10 ratings.

When it rates hospitals, for example, it examines risk-adjusted death rates and complications, based on millions of discharge records. It not only surveys patients about hospitals but doctors too.

The main problem—and it's a big one—is that Consumers' Checkbook is available for only seven metropolitan areas: Chicago, Boston, Philadelphia, Seattle, San Francisco, Minneapolis-St. Paul, and Washington, D.C. However, its ratings of doctors, hospitals, and health plans are for metro areas nationwide.

- **Angie's List.** A nearly nationwide reviewer of services is Angie's List, found at www.angieslist.com. Its subscription fees vary depending on home region.

Membership to the service includes access to the Web site, a monthly magazine, and a phone-in service if you want a staffer to search the site for you. It also offers a complaint-resolution service, where Angie's List personnel will try to help resolve a dispute with a service vendor.

Whereas Consumers' Checkbook is deep with information, Angie's List is wide, covering 120 metropolitan areas and 300 categories of service. Angie's List ratings are based on user reviews. It lists every report online for you to read, rather than only compiling results into ratings. The service does not allow anonymous reporting, it reviews reports that go into the system, and it limits the number of times consumers can report on a company.

A potential drawback is that Angie's List has a relationship with some service providers, including allowing companies to respond to negative user reports and selling highly rated companies the right to offer discount coupons on the site. For usability and credibility, though, Angie's List is superior to free Web sites that offer ratings of service companies.

- **Free Web sites.** The upside of free-ratings Web sites is they don't cost anything. But they are probably the most unreliable too. That's especially true if reviews are anonymous and unregulated. That makes it easy for companies to submit fake positive reviews about themselves or negative reviews of competitors, for example.

Because they're free, however, they're worth checking. But take ratings with a grain of salt. Examples of sites are Yelp.com, CitySearch.com, and AOL Yellow Pages. Service-specific sites include TripAdvisor.com for travel-related reviews, ServiceMagic.com for home improvement, and WebMD.com for medical reviews.

- **The Franklin Report.** Franklinreport.com offers recommended home-improvement providers in New York, Chicago, Los Angeles, Connecticut-Westchester County, N.Y., and Southeast Florida.

Other good resources include the Better Business Bureau, state licensing agencies, and state and local consumer affairs offices. For some national chain service providers, try sites I already mentioned for products, ConsumerReports.org and ConsumerSearch.com.

To keep it simple, subscribe to Consumers' Checkbook if you live in one of the covered regions. Otherwise, subscribe to Angie's List.

2. Research Prices

Granted, this advice is as old as the hills, but you really should get three price quotes, especially for expensive services.

Is $18,000 a good price for re-siding your house? You really have no idea until you get multiple quotes. Is it reasonable to pay $80 a month for a gym membership? It depends on what you get, right? Maybe for you the YMCA is a better deal than Gold's Gym, LA Fitness, or Bally Total Fitness.

I could write a whole other book on finding travel deals. But you should especially compare prices on the staples of airline tickets, hotel rates, and rental cars—and to some extent, cruises.

The Internet can help here too. Check the big online travel sites such as Expedia.com, Orbitz.com, and Travelocity.com. But you might find better flights and fares at such aggregation sites as Kayak.com, which searches 200 sites, and Mobissimo.com, which might be better for international flights. Both sites also search hotel and car-rental rates. If you don't know whether to book a flight now or later, check out Farecast.com, which helps you predict whether ticket prices to your route will be going up or down. You can bid for rates at Priceline.com and Hotwire.com. For travel reviews, see TripAdvisor.com.

The point of getting multiple price quotes is to know what the range of prices is. That's fundamental to being a smart spender.

Be Afraid of Commitment

One of the biggest consumer traps comes from subscription services. That includes a book-of-the-month club, satellite radio service for the car, a fitness club membership, or even your pay television service.

Automatic payments—often monthly payments—are insidious because they use inertia. Once you sign up for an automatically renewing service, it's way too easy to let it continue, even if you don't want the service anymore. Unless you're ultradisciplined, you probably have one of these automatic-payment spending regrets in your past—and probably, you have one on your credit card bill right now.

It's understandable. We're busy people. But it's worth going through your credit card statement and automatic bank debits to find some services that you should eliminate. If a service is worth it to you, by all means, continue it. But chances are you'll find something to cut out that you won't miss.

The problem is that we, as consumers, are far too optimistic about how much we'll use services when we sign up. Marketers of services know this about us. That's why they always break down payments into easy installments, usually monthly. Sometimes, they go further, citing the price as "less than a dollar a day," instead of $350.

When considering a service, be wary of long-term commitments and choose a la carte or per-use pricing at first—until you know how often you'll use the service. And convert the monthly cost to an annual cost, which seems to put it in better perspective. The $80-per-month gym membership doesn't sound so cheap when expressed as nearly $1,000 a year.

By the way, automatic spending is bad for the exact reason that automatic savings is good. You do it without thinking.

3. Reevaluate and Review Contracts Carefully

As with products, you want to avoid impulse buys you later regret. So, unless it's an emergency, like a broken pipe flooding your house, take your time.

Make the effort to read through contracts for bigger jobs. If it's an especially large project, like a major home renovation, you might want to have an attorney review the contract.

QUICK TIP

Try haggling. Especially with services, the price isn't always the price. Sometimes, you can get a better price just by asking for a "best and final" quote. With products, ask for a better deal if you're buying multiple expensive items at the same time, such as a refrigerator and dishwasher or a whole room full of furniture. The more knowledgeable, firm, and aggressive you are, the more likely you will succeed.

How to Buy Online

Buying online can be a great idea. What's more convenient than sitting at your computer in your pajamas, clicking the computer mouse and having the item show up on your doorstep a few days later?

Virtually all retailers that have brick-and-mortar stores also have online stores. If you haven't tried online shopping, give it a shot, at least for a small purchase. You're likely to become hooked on how easy it is.

How to Buy Online, 1-2-3

1. **Prefer commodities.**
2. **Consider shipping cost versus sales tax.**
3. **Use a credit card.**

For those of you who are experts at shopping online, I'm sure you'll excuse me if I go over some basics for people who have never tried it.

Online shopping is similar to catalog shopping, in that you choose items you want, pay for them, and they're shipped to you. With online shopping, you usually identify items you want to order by clicking on a "buy" button and placing them in a virtual shopping cart. Then, as if you were in a real store, you proceed to a "checkout" screen. There, you provide payment and shipping information. And you're done. Often, you'll get an e-mail that confirms the transaction.

Of course, the top question asked by shoppers who haven't made a purchase on the Internet is, "Is online shopping safe?" To which, I'd have to respond, "Compared with what?"

If some computer hacker were to somehow intercept your credit card number in mid-transaction—highly unlikely—so what? When the thief makes an illegal purchase, you call your credit card company and cancel the card. The bank will issue you a new card and waive any fraudulent charges. You take just as great a risk every time you hand a restaurant waiter your credit card and he disappears with it to a backroom cash register. How hard would it be for the waiter to copy down the number and use it elsewhere?

Most online transactions are encrypted, meaning they're secure. When checking out, look at the Web address in your browser. It's secure if it says https: instead of http:. You can also look for a padlock icon in your Web browser, which signifies a secure site.

If you're worried about not getting merchandise you paid for, you can stick with merchants you've heard of. And, as discussed later in this section, if you use a credit card, you probably have further consumer protections offered by your card company.

If you're worried about your name, address, and telephone number being misused, well, you might be shocked at how easy it is to get that information anyway. I'm not saying that's OK; just that online shopping doesn't add much to that risk.

1. Prefer Commodities

For the uninitiated, online shopping is best for products that are commodities, in the sense that they are identical no matter where you buy them. They're widely available and it makes no difference which copy of the article you buy.

Sure, you can buy shoes and custom-made furniture online, but you don't get to touch, try on, and thoroughly examine online products. That's a drawback for some purchases.

Early on in electronic commerce, books on Amazon.com were among the first products sold. They were ideal to purchase on the Internet because each copy of a new book is exactly the same. The same was true of music CDs.

In a narrower sense, the Internet can be good for the opposite—finding uncommon things, such as antiques and oddball merchandise. That's because the market-place is so much larger than you will find in any one region of the country.

But especially if you're just getting started with online shopping, opt for commodities.

QUICK TIP

When buying from an unfamiliar site, look for an "About Us" page, and do a quick Google search on the retailer's name, looking for other customers' experiences. Some comparison shopbots rate retailers. If the retailer has a privacy policy, all the better.

---

2. Consider Shipping Cost Versus Sales Tax

The biggest drawback to ordering online is the item has to be shipped to you. That means you'll have to wait a few days, which a lot of us aren't very good at. More important, you often have to pay shipping and handling charges.

You'll find some listings have a very low price for the product, but exorbitant shipping fees. This happens a lot on auction site eBay.com. Bulky and heavy items, such as televisions, can cost more than $100 to ship.

In the end, all you should care about is the total price. So, always add together both components of an online purchase—the purchase price, plus shipping and handling. Often, you'll find online prices to be so much lower that it's still cheaper to buy online, even if you have to pay for shipping and handling.

One advantage of online shopping is you won't necessarily have to pay state sales tax on the purchase. If the retailer has no locations in your state, it is not required to collect sales tax on checkout. Technically, most states require you to pay sales tax on Internet purchases, presumably by keeping track of purchases and accounting for the tax on your state income tax form. But almost nobody does that, which essentially makes Internet purchases from out-of-state retailers cheaper.

I'm not saying that avoiding state sales tax on Internet purchases is right or wrong. I'm just saying that's how it is. Still, this is a fluid issue, as state governments try to fill their coffers by collecting sales-tax money from Internet sales. So, stay tuned.

3. Use a Credit Card

Use a credit card for online transactions because the consumer protections are so much stronger than for debit cards. This is especially true if you're dealing with unfamiliar sellers.

A big benefit of using a credit card is its dispute service. If you have a problem with the Internet merchant and can't get it resolved, pass the dispute on to your credit card company and allow them to battle the retailer for you.

Further, if someone at that retailer misuses your card and starts making purchases with it, you're not liable for them. By federal law, you're liable for $50, but all the major credit card companies limit your liability to zero.

Of course, these protections apply whether you're shopping online or in a real store. But online you have a greater chance of dealing with an unfamiliar retailer. Credit cards are a buffer between you and a strange merchant.

For more about credit cards, see Chapter 6, "Credit When Credit's Due."

One exception to this rule is if you don't own a credit card and don't want to. Maybe you've gotten into trouble before running up balances you had trouble paying off. In that case, you're left with using your debit card that acts as a Visa or MasterCard.

Other intermediary forms of online payment, such as PayPal and Google Checkout, can link to credit cards and bank accounts. But they're not widely available as payment options.

QUICK TIP

Get an autofill program. These little computer programs will fill in your name and address information and some even store your credit card information, so you don't have to fetch your card each time you buy something online. Just as valuable, these programs automatically fill in your logins and passwords to all the different retailers you buy from. There are some free autofill programs available, often as plug-ins for Web browsers, such as Google Toolbar, toolbar.google.com. I shop online so often, I bought a robust form filler called RoboForm Pro, www.roboform.com (Windows only).

Coupon Codes and Rebate Portals

Consider these two shopping scenarios that illustrate ways to save money while shopping online.

Coupon Codes

Imagine standing at a store checkout. To get 10 percent off your order, all you would have to do is step away from the cashier for a moment and look on a nearby shelf for a coupon. Would you bother?

That's essentially what you can do while shopping on the Internet. Get in the habit of searching for discount codes, also called promotional codes or coupons.

When buying online, you place items in a virtual shopping cart and then go through a checkout procedure. While checking out, the Web site often will ask if you have a discount code to enter. These codes are generally a series of numbers and letters that unlock goodies, such as a percentage discount on your order, dollars off your purchase, and discounted or free shipping.

If you don't have a discount code, don't just ignore the promotional code box. Go code hunting.

Open a separate window in your Web browser. Call up a few of your favorite Web search engines to find codes. Type in the retailer's name, the word "code" and other terms such as "promotional," "coupon," and "discount." You can also try code aggregators, such as CouponMom.com, CouponCabin.com, FlamingoWorld.com, and CouponMountain.com. If you find a code, return to your checkout browser and type or paste the found promotional code into the box. The code might have expired, but there's no harm in trying it. The worst that happens is the retailer rejects the code. If you type in a correct code, the discount will be applied to your order.

A few minutes of searching could yield worthwhile savings, such as 10 percent off, free shipping, or $15 off an order, for example.

Rebate Portals

Imagine you're standing at the threshold of a retail store, but you can get a 10 percent discount if you walk through another entry door. Would you do it?

That's what you can do by shopping through rebate portals.

A shopping portal, or entrance, is a separate free Web site that has an arrangement with retailers. Retailers pay a commission to portal operators in return for sending Internet consumer traffic to the retailer's site—a kind of referral fee. When the consumer makes a purchase, the retailer pays the portal a commission. A "rebate" shopping portal goes a step further and shares its commission with the consumer.

To use a rebate portal, sign up for free at the portal's site. Then, instead of making a purchase directly at a retailer's Web site, go to the portal to see whether it is affiliated with that retailer. If so, click the link to enter the retailer through a side door, of sorts. Then, proceed through the online checkout as you normally would.

Behind the scenes, the retailer knows the portal sent you. It pays a commission to the portal. Then the portal shares the commission with you by crediting your portal rebate account. It's all electronic and automatic, akin to a rewards credit card.

A typical rebate to you would be about 5 percent of the purchase price, but it can vary widely, even surpassing 10 percent for some retailers. Opt for cash rebates instead of points or other rewards.

Popular rewards sites include FatWallet.com, Ebates.com, Jellyfish.com, and QuickRewards. net. Portals that donate your rewards to college savings plans include Upromise.com, BabyMint. com, and LittleGrad.com. If you're having trouble choosing, go with Ebates.com. Learn more at CompareRewards.com.

Fun Tangent: Eyeglasses Online

You can buy almost anything online nowadays. One of my favorites is eyeglasses. Weird, right?

The short story is my first pair of glasses purchased online cost me $8. Actually, with shipping and a clip-on sun shade, they cost $16.90 delivered. I see great with them and they look good too. In fact, it's a toss-up which I like more, these glasses or the ones I paid about $300 for from a chain-store optician.

I ordered them from ZenniOptical.com.

Granted, there are no frills with ordering glasses this way. They arrived in seven business days in a padded envelope in a simple hard-plastic case.

There are a few minor drawbacks:

1. My written prescription from my eye doctor did not include a measurement for PD, pupillary distance, which is basically the distance in millimeters between the centers of your eyeballs. You need this measurement to order online. I measured my PD in a mirror. I'm sure that's not the way the eye doctor would recommend, but it seems to have worked.

2. You might have to have the nose pads and arms of the glasses adjusted if they don't sit right on your face. This might cost you a few bucks, but many optometrists will do it for free.

3. The clip-on sun shade isn't custom-made for the glasses, but it fits and covers the lenses well.

The cheap glasses have thinner metal and might not last as long. However, doing the math, I can buy 16 pairs of ZenniOptical glasses for the price of one discounted pair at a popular retailer. At these prices, you can own several different styles of eyeglasses for a fraction of the usual retail price.

I was so pleased I followed up by ordering rimless bifocals with every option available, including antireflective coating. That surely would have cost $500 at an optician or eye doctor. My cost: $68. My 10-year-old son now refuses to wear his $300 eyeglasses, and insists on wearing his $8 Zennis. He says he just likes them better. Go figure.

By the way, a different Web site, EyeBuyDirect.com, also sells eyeglasses for about $8.

How to Buy Used Stuff

Buying used stuff can elicit extreme opinions, usually from people who rarely, if ever, buy anything second-hand. But buying every item in your life as new just isn't being smart with money.

Maybe nowhere is the argument for buying used items more persuasive than in buying cars. New cars can lose 30 percent of their value in the first year of ownership. So, if you're talking about a $30,000 vehicle, the difference between a new car and 1-year-old car is $9,000. If $9,000 is a lot of money in your world, this discussion about buying used stuff is for you.

How to Buy Used Stuff, 1-2-3

1. **Get over the "yuck" factor.**
2. **Evaluate price and quality.**
3. **Keep it simple.**

---

1. Get Over the "Yuck" Factor

The first step in saving money with used items is to break through a mental barrier. It might not be pleasant to read it in black and white, but some people think used merchandise is:

- Broken/tattered
- Dirty/smelly
- Not worth my time/Only for poor people

So, I'm here to tell you that buying something used doesn't make you an inferior person. I don't think of myself as generally inferior, and I'm not poor. But I regularly stop by a local consignment shop to see what men's clothing they have. I bought a suit for $25 that I wear during television appearances. I bought a pullover windbreaker for $2. I splurged on two pricey silk neckties, $8 each.

How do you get over a mental barrier about buying used? Just do it.

This is another of the rare occasions where I advise you to spend money to save money. Go to a local thrift store or consignment shop and buy a used piece of clothing that you will wear, even if it's only a scarf or belt. Alternatively, buy a set of drinking glasses or plates. The point is to buy something used that you have a very personal interaction with. This way, you can confront your fears about buying used merchandise. If you have a pleasant experience, your aversion to buying used stuff will dissipate, if not disappear. You will get over the "yuck" factor.

Then a whole new world of retail opens up to you. You can consider used items from eBay.com, Craigslist.com, Freecycle.org, garage sales, flea markets, thrift stores, and newspaper classified ads.

QUICK TIP

Add to your barrier-breaking errands a stop by a local dollar store. The merchandise isn't used, but it is cheap. Dollar stores can be ideal outlets for junk food, such as cookies, pretzels, and chips. I've bought such things as an iPod case, calculator, greeting cards, and printer USB cord at a dollar store. Just avoid cheap electric or electronic items for fear of a fire hazard.

2. Evaluate Price and Quality

Buying something used might mean settling for a product of lower quality than you can get new. That's fine for many purchases. Nobody can reasonably expect to buy the best of everything.

On the other hand, buying used might mean you can afford something of *higher* quality. If you have $500 to spend on a living room sofa, which do you think is higher quality: a new one from Ikea or an Ethan Allen model purchased used? So buying used sometimes means you can get a superior product.

Similarly, buying used might get you a luxury brand with more features. Go back to the automobile example. Would you rather have a 2009 Chevrolet Cobalt subcompact or a 2-year-old Honda Accord? Or, for that matter, a 2003 Lexus ES 300 or BMW 3 Series? They all cost the same.

But, it's true, buying used items can be more of a hassle than buying new. So, it's always important to evaluate prices and quality.

3. Keep It Simple

Some items are not functionally different whether new or used, assuming they are undamaged. These include movie DVDs, music CDs, video games, and, yes, even books like this one. A simple garden shovel or hammer is preferable to buy used, rather than a rototiller or circular saw. The simpler, the better—fewer things to go wrong.

Other examples of great used purchases include kids clothing, toys, and musical instruments—considering they might be used for a short time. Consider simple sports equipment, such as golf clubs, assuming you're not worried about custom fitting.

Of course, automobiles don't exactly fit into the category of a "simple" machine. But cars are so reliable nowadays. Many go 150,000 miles with only routine maintenance. So a corollary of the "simple" rule is to favor used items when they're reliable.

QUICK TIP

An often overlooked source of free used items is your local public library. Besides books, many have a wide variety of periodicals, movie videos, and music CDs.

Refurbished Electronics

One way to purchase electronics cheaper is to buy them as "refurbished." Contrary to its name, refurbished often does not mean the item is used, repaired, or inferior in quality. In fact, it might undergo tighter quality control than a new item because someone has checked to make sure the machine works.

The reason an item is classified as a "refurb" could be minor, such as marred packaging. Or, maybe a previous customer bought the item but returned it because he didn't like the color or couldn't figure out how to use it.

Consumer savings from buying refurbs can be significant, 10 percent to 50 percent off retail price.

I've done even better than that. I bought a refurbished universal remote control that operates a TV and several related components. It's a fancy remote—definitely falls in the "wants" category. It typically costs about $150. I got a refurbished one for $80. Works great. The only difference is the refurbished remote came in plain packaging instead of the colorful blister-pack the new item comes in.

However, before buying a refurb, investigate how the retailer defines "refurbished." And find out about the return policy and what warranty you'll get.

The safest place to buy a refurb is from a manufacturer. Such major makers as Dell, Apple, HP, Sony, and Epson sell their own refurbished electronics. The easiest way to search for and buy refurbs is online, often at a manufacturer's own site. Some third-party online retailers, such as TigerDirect.com and NewEgg.com, also do a robust refurb business. Major retailer Target has started selling "pre-owned electronics," and Amazon.com sells refurbs at a companion Web site, Warehousedeals.com.

How to Teach Kids about Money

Teaching children to be good spenders and savers is a topic that can befuddle even the most well-intentioned and well-informed parents. The main tool is an allowance system, which can teach skills kids will use for the rest of their lives.

As those children mature into adults, they will have to resist almost constant marketing pitches from advertisers on TV, Web sites, billboards, magazines, and newspapers. And they'll probably have credit available to them, allowing them to buy even when they can't afford it.

Money troubles await children who don't learn that money is finite, and they have to make trade-off decisions with purchases. They'll have to distinguish between needs and wants.

How to Teach Kids about Money, 1-2-3

1. **Give children an allowance.**
2. **Don't tie allowance to chores.**
3. **Make rules.**

1. Give Children an Allowance

Customize allowance amounts to what you can afford and what you think your child can handle. But don't give too little. The child needs to be able to save enough money in a relatively short period to buy something he or she wants.

A suggestion: Beginning around the ages of 5 to 7, give 50 cents per week for each year old the child is. At age 10, give $1 per year old. A less-accelerated plan is $1 weekly for each school grade level.

2. Don't Tie Allowance to Chores

Don't confuse money lessons. Learning how to spend smart as a consumer is a different lesson than "you have to work for a living." You are not paying your children a salary; you're giving them money as a tool for learning, like you would give them a piano to practice on or flash cards with which to memorize multiplication tables.

So don't tie allowance to chores. Chores are to be done by the child for free because he or she is part of the household and has a responsibility to help operate it. If a child decides she doesn't feel like doing chores and will forgo the allowance, the allowance system crumbles and the lessons are lost. How will you respond when you tell her to make her bed and she asks, "How much are you going to pay me?"

To instill a work ethic and entrepreneurial spirit, offer a list of optional jobs a child can choose to complete for extra money.

If you disagree with this philosophy, go ahead and tie allowance to chores—after all, you're the parent. But regularly talk to the child about both lessons—spending and earning—separately.

3. Make Rules

Require the child to earmark money each pay period for three accounts: spending, saving, and giving. For younger children, it's easy to place equal amounts into three containers or envelopes, labeled with each category. Identify types of purchases the child will be responsible for. Don't give loans or advances.

The "spending" account is where all the action is, and some of the best lessons. Money in this account should be spent regularly.

Allow children to make mistakes with this money. You want them to buy things impulsively that they later regret. You want them to buy a poor-quality item that breaks. You want them to run out of money, forcing them to save for several weeks to buy the next thing. You want them to choose among similar items with different prices.

Children need the repetition of buying things and witnessing the consequences of the decisions. Of course, parents should retain veto power over types of purchases, such as candy or dangerous toys.

Regularly talking to children after money decisions, especially poor spending decisions, is crucial. Talk about your own money life, too, such as why you're using coupons at the supermarket and how credit cards work.

With the "saving" account, the point is to show how money adds up over time. This money is not to be spent but to be counted and monitored. When you dismantle the allowance system in the child's late teens, the money can be used for college expenses or a car, for example.

Earmarking money for "giving"—weekly church donations or periodic donations to a charity—provides a deeper lesson about what money can be used for.

Of course, you can adjust the allowance plan to fit lessons you are trying to teach. Here are examples:

- Include lunch money in older children's allowance and offer a deal: The children can keep the lunch money for each day they make a lunch at home and brown-bag it.
- Switch to a monthly allowance for older children, forcing them to budget their money over a longer period.
- Make saving optional but offer to match the child's contribution to their savings dollar for dollar.

Details of an allowance system aren't as important as making the effort to start one, adjusting it over time and teaching the lessons.

Chapter 5

Green Means Green

B y now, we all know the "inconvenient truth"—
the Earth's environment is endangered. But here's
a convenient truth: You can help Mother Earth
while saving money.

Links between environmentalism and spending
smart are undeniable. You don't have to look hard to
see that going green means more green in your neigh-
borhood and in your wallet. It's a realization corporate
America is just now waking up to. Such terms as *sus-
tainability* and *carbon footprint* have entered the board-
room lexicon.

For consumers, the primary misconception is that
making an environmental effort will cost you money or
convenience. That can be true in some cases. But today,
there are many examples of how you can save green
while going green.

This chapter gives just a few examples of the easiest
and most worthwhile steps to take.

Gasoline

No other price fires up Americans more than gasoline prices. Maybe it's because we have no control over prices and feel helpless. Maybe it's because it's a necessary expense, especially in suburban and rural areas. Or maybe it's because we see the prices flaunted in huge numbers at every commercial traffic intersection.

Whatever the reason, you can probably spend less on gas. That not only puts more money back in your pocket but helps the environment and America's dependence on foreign oil.

Gasoline, 1-2-3

1. **Don't spill the coffee.**
2. **Take it slow and steady.**
3. **Pump it up.**

A discussion about saving on gas centers on two main areas: *What* you drive and *how* you drive.

Let's start with what you drive.

Many people think they can fix their gas-spending problem by trading in their gas-guzzler for a new fuel-efficient car. That's often false. The reason? Hidden costs.

We won't get into all the math here, but depreciation of a new vehicle and the cost of financing that vehicle often far surpasses any gasoline savings you'll reap. So, unless you're accounting for those hidden costs, you can't accurately assess the value of swapping vehicles.

Other hidden costs include higher insurance rates for a newer car and sales tax that you'll have to pay if you live in a state that levies sales tax. Let's look at sales tax alone. At 6 percent, you'll pay $1,500 in sales tax to buy a $25,000 vehicle. $1,500 buys a lot of gas for your gas-guzzler.

Now, if you were going to replace your current vehicle anyway, it makes sense to buy a fuel-efficient one. Of course, the best idea is to buy a late-model used car, which allows someone else to take the tremendous first-year depreciation hit of a new car.

So, for saving money on gasoline, that leaves us with *how* you drive.

1. Don't Spill the Coffee

While driving, imagine you have a cup of coffee, uncovered, in your cup holder. You don't want that coffee to slosh out of the cup and onto you or the car floor. So, what do you do? You try to drive as smoothly as possible, with gradual acceleration, more coasting, and gradual braking. If you're accustomed to being aggressive with the accelerator and brake pedals, this tip will improve your gas mileage considerably, making your gas dollars go further.

When automotive Web site Edmunds.com set out to prove which gas-savings tips saved the most money, they found aggressive driving was the number one money drain. Moderating your driving habits with slower acceleration and braking saved up to 37 percent on gas, with the average savings at 31 percent. Could you imagine saving one-third of the money you spend annually on gasoline? If you normally spend $50 a week to put gas in your car, that's a savings of $858 a year. Two cars? That's more than $1,700 saved.

Smooth acceleration, cornering, and braking extend the life of the engine, transmission, brakes, and tires, too, saving even more money.

2. Take It Slow and Steady

Here's another visualization that might work. Imagine that as you press down on the accelerator pedal, money leaks from your wallet. The harder you press, the more money leaks out. It's like at the gas station when you begin fueling up your vehicle: The tighter you squeeze the trigger of the fuel pump, the faster the price-readout advances.

The point is to drive slower.

Consumer Reports tested a Toyota Camry. By increasing the highway cruising speed from 55 mph to 65, the car's fuel economy dropped from 40 miles per gallon to 35. Speeding up to 75 mph cost the car another 5 mpg. One reason, *Consumer Reports* says, is that aerodynamic drag increases exponentially the faster you drive. It simply takes more fuel to power the car through the air.

And use cruise control when you can, even on sub-urban roads at 40 mph. It's a surprisingly effective way to save gas, up to 14 percent, Edmunds.com found. Cruise control smoothes out the driver's accelerator use, preventing surges. It also makes the driver take the long view of the road, rather than reacting to every change in traffic around them.

3. Pump It Up

OK, I'll concede that keeping your car tires properly inflated is a common tip and it won't save you tons of money or gasoline. But it's so cheap and easy.

Consumer Reports found a Toyota Camry experienced a 1.3 mpg loss in highway fuel economy when tires were underinflated by 10 pounds per square inch (psi). Maybe more important, underinflated tires compromise handling and braking and wear faster. Underinflated tires also run much hotter, which can lead to tire failure.

Check the pressure of your vehicle's tires at least once a month with a tire gauge. The correct pressure usually can be found on a label in your vehicle's driver-side door jamb. Of course, you'll want to keep an eye out for a service station that doesn't charge for using its tire pump.

Gasoline Myths

Some bad information gets passed around about saving money on gas. Here are a few examples:

- **Air conditioning versus open windows.** This has been a long-running debate, but the short answer is there's no significant difference in fuel economy. Do whatever makes you more comfortable.

- **Additives and devices.** Don't bother with fuel-tank additives and devices that attach to your vehicle. They claim to improve your gas mileage. But they don't work. The U.S. Environmental Protection Agency and *Consumer Reports* have tested them. None of these additives and devices makes much difference in fuel economy.

- **Morning fill-ups.** A common tip is to fill your gas tank in the morning, when the fuel is cool, rather than in the heat of the day. The theory is that the cooler gasoline will be denser, so you will get more for your money. But the temperature of the gasoline coming out of the fuel nozzle changes very little, if at all, during any 24-hour stretch. Any extra gas you get will be negligible, *Consumer Reports* says.

Home Heating and Cooling

Most energy savings in your home will come in one of two ways: You can take steps that allow you to adjust the thermostat and use less energy or, keeping the thermostat the same, you need your furnace and air conditioner to turn on less often, mostly by keeping your paid-for air indoors longer.

Those sound like simple concepts, but they are fundamental to saving money and energy.

Home Heating and Cooling, 1-2-3

1. Make a thermostat plan.
2. Seal leaks.
3. Avoid big-ticket fixes.

1. Make a Thermostat Plan

Many of the usual tips about home heating and cooling are useless unless they allow you to do one simple thing: Adjust the thermostat to use less heat and air conditioning.

Call a meeting of everyone in your household and devise a plan for controlling temperature in your home. Agree on what times of day you can set the thermostat really low in the winter—without risk of freezing pipes, of course. While you're home, can you set the temperature at 68 degrees instead of 72 if everyone in the household agrees to wear sweaters and slippers around the house? Can you be comfortable at 66 degrees? Will flannel pajamas and an extra blanket on the bed allow you to lower the temperature into the 50s at night? If someone is home all day, make it a routine to open drapes to let the sun's heat in and otherwise close drapes to help further insulate windows.

The opposite is true in summer. When can you use less air conditioning and allow the house to get warmer? Will everybody agree to wear light clothing to reduce the need for cooling? Will everybody be conscious about when it's bearable to open windows to get a breeze rather than use air conditioning?

These steps seem obvious to me and they might to you too. But ask yourself why on so many gorgeous spring or fall days at perfectly comfortable temperatures so many of your neighbors have their windows closed and heat or air conditioning running? Somebody is not getting the message or there are a lot of people who close up their homes because they suffer from outdoor allergies.

If your household is undisciplined about turning the thermostat up and down and has a routine schedule, buy an Energy Star-rated programmable thermostat. This device is easy to install and costs about $100. It's basically just a timer that sets your thermostat to a pre-scribed temperature at various times during the day and night. For example, you could let the house get warm in the summer while you're at work and start cooling it before you arrive home. You could make back the cost of the $100 programmable thermostat in one year's worth of energy savings. However, if you're diligent about controlling temperature the old-fashioned way— by walking over to the thermostat and setting it by hand—you don't need a programmable thermostat.

This adjusting of the thermostat won't work unless people in the household—or at least those who control the temperature—are on board with the plan.

2. Seal Leaks

This too seems like obvious advice, but you have to actually take the time to find and seal leaks. That's so you can keep your paid-for air indoors longer.

Walk the exterior perimeter of your home to look for cracks and unsealed seams, not only around windows and doors, but in pipe cutouts to the outdoors, chimneys, and the foundation.

Indoors, carefully hold a candle, stick of incense, or other flame near seams in your windows and exterior doors. If the flame and smoke blow, you know you have a leak. Caulking, weather-stripping, and foam sealant will plug those leaks.

Also check recessed lights, baseboards, electrical outlets to exterior walls, and unfinished spaces behind cupboards and closets.

Seal leaky air ducts at joints, starting at the furnace air handler, and insulate ducts that run through unheated basements or attics. In a typical house, about 20 percent of the air that moves through the duct system is lost due to leaks and poorly sealed connections, according to the federal government's Energy Star program. But duct tape isn't the answer. It's actually a poor way to seal duct cracks and seams. Use a mashed potato-like sealant called mastic. Or use the water-based kind. You paint it on duct joints and tiny holes, and it hardens. You could also use metallic duct tape with a UL-181 rating. Search the EnergyStar.gov site for the online brochure, "Duct Sealing."

Use appropriate insulation for your climate. It can increase your comfort and reduce your heating costs up to 30 percent. Start with attic insulation, followed by exterior and basement walls, floors, and crawl spaces. Learn more about insulating at www.simplyinsulate. com. Also, see the publication "A Do-it-Yourself Guide to Energy Star Home Sealing" by the Environmental Protection Agency. Call 1-888-782-7937 or get it online at EnergyStar.gov.

3. Avoid Big-Ticket Fixes

Always calculate the breakeven point for any energy-savings effort. For example, replacing old windows will save energy, but they're so expensive it might take decades before you earn back enough in energy savings to pay for the windows. The same goes for replacing a functioning furnace or central air-conditioning unit.

If you're upgrading or replacing for other nonmonetary reasons, such as the attractivness of the windows or because you want to help preserve the environment, that's fine. Just know what it's actually costing you.

Little Things Mean a Lot

So much of what we can do to save money and the environment doesn't come via grand one-time efforts, but through our daily habits.

Little Things Mean a Lot, 1-2-3

1. Replace your five most-used bulbs with CFLs (compact fluorescent lamps).
2. Buy rechargeable batteries.
3. Don't buy bottled water.

1. Replace Your Five Most-Used Bulbs with CFLs

I was watching a TV rerun of the sitcom *Friends* when the inferiority of the traditional incandescent light bulbs struck me. The character Monica, a chef on the show, was reminiscing that as a child she cooked with an Easy-Bake Oven.

The child's toy Easy-Bake Oven bakes cookies and cakes with a 100-watt incandescent light bulb. Think about that. The Easy-Bake Oven is possible because traditional light bulbs are actually small heaters that happen to give off some light. They are wildly inefficient ways to illuminate a room. It's 130-year-old technology.

Meanwhile, compact fluorescent lamps, CFLs, are so much better than they used to be. They're definitely worth a try.

Each CFL will save you $30 to $50 over its life, compared with an incandescent bulb. That's because CFLs use one-quarter of the electricity. The energy savings more than make up for the higher purchase price. And they last 10 times longer than incandescents. I bought CFLs that say on the package they are guaranteed to last nine years—not nine months—nine years.

How's the quality? Quite good, actually. Problems with flickering, humming, and giving off poor color light have all been remedied. Lights might turn on a little slowly and take several seconds to get to full brightness. But I don't find that to be a big problem. In fact, it's less jarring than having immediate brightness.

The important point here is to at least try them. Start by replacing bulbs in your five most-used lights. The best deals are buying multipacks of CFLs at warehouse clubs and home centers.

Avoid putting CFLs in lights with dimmer switches. Though some CFLs are made for dimmable lights, the bulbs lag behind in quality compared with incandescent. The biggest problem is the range of dimming, which is narrow. It's like having a dimming range of full, half, and off, rather than all the brightness levels in between.

A minor environmental drawback of CFLs is they contain a tiny amount of mercury. It's best not to throw them in the trash. Instead, go online to Earth911.org to find out where to drop them off for disposal. As of this writing, a few national retailers, such as Home Depot and RadioShack, will take them.

CFLs are really just a transitional technology, until we get LED (light-emitting diode) bulbs, which use even less power, last longer, give off better light, and don't have the mercury problem. But we're not there yet. Until we are, CFLs are a great way to go.

QUICK TIP

Another way to save electricity is to kill the vampires. Vampire appliances are neither fully on, nor fully off, existing in a kind of undead state. Examples of vampires are computers, DVD players, VCRs, TVs, battery chargers, and cable and satellite TV boxes.

They secretly suck electricity, day and night, even when powered off. This "standby loss" bleeds dollars from your wallet and wastes electricity. Did you know that over its life, a microwave oven consumes more energy powering its clock than it does cooking food?

For electronics grouped together, use a power strip,
which allows you to flip a switch on the strip to cut
all power to the components.

2. Buy Rechargeable Batteries

Like CFLs, rechargeable batteries have gotten a lot better recently. They're worth trying because you can save money and avoid a lot of AA and AAA batteries and their packaging ending up in landfills.

Rechargeable batteries are more expensive up front, but far cheaper over the long run, even factoring in the cost of the charger and minimal electricity used. And today, rechargeables last longer on a charge than a regular disposable alkaline.

The big drawback had always been that traditional rechargeable batteries lose battery power while idle. So, if your digital camera has been sitting in a drawer for a few months, its rechargeable batteries could be drained when you need it to capture an unexpected great moment.

Enter the new breed of rechargeables, called hybrids or precharged batteries. These nickel metal hydride (NiMH) cells come already charged and lose power at a slow rate, maintaining 85 percent of their charge, even after sitting idle for a year. You can recharge batteries literally hundreds of times.

Here's how four rechargeable AA batteries could save you nearly $2,000.

Four AA rechargeable batteries that yielded 500 charges each would cost $50, including the cost of the charger. Electricity cost for charging is negligible, literally a few pennies.

The equivalent would be buying 2,000 disposable batteries. At $1 each, that's $2,000.

Net savings is $1,950.

I bought a brand that was one of the pioneers in the hybrid rechargeables, the Sanyo Eneloop. They work quite well. They're especially good for devices that eat through batteries, such as computer mice, video-game controllers, and cameras.

You should recycle rechargeables. Fortunately, it's easy. You can drop them off at such retailers as Sears, RadioShack, Home Depot, Lowe's, Staples, and OfficeMax. See call2recycle.org for a list of battery recyclers near you.

QUICK TIP

Whether you use disposables or rechargeable batteries, it makes sense to invest in a battery tester. Some are as cheap as $5. A voltmeter or battery tester can determine which in a group of batteries is the dud, so you don't have to replace all batteries in a multibattery device.

3. Don't Buy Bottled Water

There's only one beverage for humans that literally falls from the sky for free. It's water. Water is the only beverage that's so common and inexpensive that you can drink as much as you want from a public fountain and nobody cares.

Yet, somehow beverage companies persuaded Americans to pay good money for a free product, all because they put it in a bottle for you. Mind you, this is a product that requires you to go to the store, load heavy cases into your shopping cart, pay real money for a virtually free product, and lug it home.

Test after test shows that bottled water does not taste better than tap water, nor is it safer from contaminants. Tap water in most parts of the United States is very high quality. In fact, much of the bottled water sold, including from brands Aquafina and Dasani, comes from municipal tap water, not mountain springs or glaciers or whatever else is pictured on the bottle's label.

If your home tap water has an off taste, filter it. A cheap pitcher-style filter works great.

If you want to spend money to drink water and make a social statement, consider drinking tap water or filtered tap water from a fancy water bottle. A quick Internet search finds several water-bottle retailers including Mysigg.com and kleankanteen.com. Bottles from NewWaveEnviro.com are made from corn and biodegrade in 80 days. Bottles from Aquamira.com and thewatergeeks.com have filters built into the bottle.

Not only is paying for bottled water hard on your pocketbook—some households spend more than

$1,000 a year—it's hard on the environment. There's making the bottle in the first place, which requires oil. Then there's emissions and fuel consumption by trucks that transport the bottled water. And then there's disposing of the bottle, many of which are not recycled.

QUICK TIP

Part of the hazard of bottled water is throwing the disposable bottle "away." The problem is: There is no "away." That points to a broader issue about usable stuff ending up in landfills. Profit from your would-be junk by selling it on eBay.com or Craigslist.com. Give it away via freecycle.org or get a tax deduction by donating to local charities or thrift shops.

Really, this advice about bottled water is a metaphor for all kinds of unnecessary spending on disposable products—plates, cups, napkins, paper towels, and a wide host of other products.

Choose to reuse. You wallet and Mother Earth will thank you.

For more energy-saving tips, go online to the Alliance to Save Energy, ase.org; the U.S. energy department's energy-efficiency site for consumers, www.eere.energy. gov/consumer; the American Council for an Energy-Efficient Economy, aceee.org; and the Energy Star program, www.energystar.gov.

Should You Buy Carbon Offsets?

A popular exercise nowadays is to measure your carbon footprint. That estimates how much you are emitting in greenhouse gases by heating your home, driving your car, and flying on airplanes, for example.

The antidote, some say, is to buy carbon offsets. A carbon offset is essentially a promise that your money will help pay for projects that reduce greenhouse gases.

The average person who puts 10 tons of carbon dioxide into the atmosphere a year might offset that impact by buying $150 worth of carbon credits. Prices vary widely. The money goes toward such projects as planting trees, building wind-power projects, and capturing and destroying methane from landfills and dairy farms. The idea is to pay for the emissions damage you cause so your existence on the planet is carbon neutral.

But as a consumer, is buying carbon credits spending smart?

I'm not a fan.

First, critics are right to fear that some people will throw money at the problem to alleviate their guilt without changing their behaviors—write a check and hop in the Hummer to go to work. Second, there are too few good ways to be sure your money is being used wisely.

Far more effective than purchasing carbon off-sets is reducing your personal consumption by using some of the tips in this chapter.

PART II

Spending Smart Yesterday

Chapter 6

Credit When Credit's Due

Credit is an increasingly important component of money management nowadays, whether you borrow money or not. That's why it's important to care about your credit reports, your credit scores, and your credit cards, if you use them.

This has never been truer since the whole financial world started to reexamine the loose lending standards that led to tumult in the financial markets in late 2008. The days of easy credit, given to anybody who can fog a mirror, are gone.

Credit scores are intended to define how creditworthy you are. Can lenders trust you to pay back borrowed money on time? That's all creditworthiness is. The more trustworthy you are, according to a credit-scoring formula, the more likely you'll get a loan in the first place and the more likely you'll get a lower interest rate than less trustworthy people.

Your Credit

Unless you've been living under a rock, you have heard about credit reports and credit scores. They're not particularly new. But in recent years, the companies you do business with use reports and scores a lot more. And, though credit reports were once-secret dossiers about your money life, consumers today have more information gathered and stored about them than ever before.

Your Credit, 1-2-3

1. **Get your credit reports.** Go online to www.AnnualCreditReport.com and retrieve your free credit reports. Dispute errors.

2. **Get your credit scores (optional).** If you'll be applying for an important loan soon, pay to get your "FICO" credit scores at www.MyFico.com.

3. **Improve your scores.** Review what goes into a credit rating and take steps to improve your FICO score.

What Is a Credit Rating?

Basically, credit reports work like this: Companies you owe money to regularly report on you to three credit bureaus named Experian, Equifax, and TransUnion.

Did you pay your bills or didn't you? They report good stuff, such as on-time car payments, and bad stuff, such as failing to pay your cell-phone bill. Information on those reports translates into point values. Those points go into a math formula that spits out a three-digit number, your credit score. Lenders and others can look at that score and decide whether they want to do business with you. If they do, the scores might determine how good a deal they're willing to offer.

The process is more complicated than that, but that's the basic idea.

Today, it's a bit shocking how vital your credit information is. Consider that raising your credit scores from the low 600s to the high 600s could save more than $5,000 a year on a 30-year, $300,000 mortgage. Meanwhile, the same rise in scores on a three-year, $25,000 auto loan could save $700 a year, according to examples from the Consumer Federation of America.

That's a huge amount of money for most people.

The problem is many consumers find credit reports and credit scores confusing—and for good reason. Some of the details seem illogical.

Did you know?

- You could earn $1 million a year and have lousy credit. Credit scores don't even consider your income, your net worth, or how much money you have in the bank.

- People who pay their credit cards off in full every month and never miss a payment could have lower credit scores than people who have late payments and collections.

- Credit bureaus and other credit companies try to trick you into buying fake scores and near-worthless monitoring services.

Unfortunately, consumers still don't seem to know much about the topic of credit reports and scores, according to annual surveys by the Consumer Federation of America. Recent survey results are shown in Figure 6.1.

According to a survey of consumers by the Consumer Federation of America:

- 31 percent of consumers know what a credit score means.

- 74 percent of people incorrectly think income affects credit scores.

- 79 percent incorrectly believe they can get their credit scores for free once a year. (They can get credit *reports* annually for free.)

Source: Consumer Federation of America survey, 2007.

FIGURE 6.1   *Understanding credit: by the numbers*

Why Your Credit Matters

Paying more than you have to because you don't understand the basics of credit scoring is just wasteful. Plugging that leak of wasteful spending will allow many people to redirect money to other priorities.

Minding your credit is important for two basic reasons: You can save a lot of money, and you can discover identity theft early.

Saving Money

As I said at the start of this chapter, credit scores attempt to define whether lenders can trust you to pay back money you've borrowed. It's not a judgment about your personal integrity. It's solely about how the credit-scoring formula tries to predict whether you'll pay back loans or pay bills on time.

Your credit scores—the only ones that matter are your three FICO scores—might even help lower your rates on home and auto insurance, or land you a job, an apartment, or a cell-phone contract. That's because insurance companies, wireless carriers, and even some employers and landlords use credit scores in their evaluations of you.

So, even if you never borrow money, your credit rating is important.

Figure 6.2 shows how much lower your monthly mortgage payment might be if you have a good credit score. A person with a lousy score would pay about $11,000 a year more than someone with a great score.

Higher FICO credit scores mean lower payments.

FICO® score	Interest rate	Monthly payment
760–850	5.82%	$1,764
700–759	6.04%	$1,807
660–699	6.33%	$1,862
620–659	7.14%	$2,024
580–619	9.45%	$2,512
500–579	10.31%	$2,702

Note: 30-year fixed mortgage rates for $300,000 loan in October 2008.
Source: MyFico.com

FIGURE 6.2 *Credit counts.*

Identity Theft

You want to know early on if a thief has stolen your identity and opened new credit accounts in your name. That's the most serious type of identity theft. As we'll discuss later, having your credit card number ripped off isn't really that big a deal.

Monitoring your credit reports lets you catch the presence of fraudulent accounts early. You might not lose a lot of money with identity theft because you have some consumer safeguards. But cleaning up the mess with banks and other creditors can be a huge hassle.

1. Get Your Credit Reports

By federal law, you're allowed to check your three credit reports for free, but generally not your credit scores. Reports are more important because they are what scores are based on. You can get a report once a year from each of the three main credit bureaus. Some state laws give you the right to get them more often.

The three credit bureaus are Experian, Equifax, and TransUnion.

Accessing Your Report

Go online to AnnualCreditReport.com, which is the only official site to get free credit reports.

Beware: The heavily advertised FreeCreditReport.com is an unconscionable attempt by the credit bureau Experian to confuse you and sell you services you don't need. Don't use that site.

Get all three reports, one from each of the three credit bureaus, if you meet the following criteria:

- This is the first time you're accessing reports.
- You will need an important loan soon.
- You have reason to believe your identity was stolen.

If this is routine credit checking, access just one report. It doesn't matter which one. Then check back every four months and access a different report. By staggering access to reports, you can check three times a year for free. Mark your calendar.

As of this writing, the procedure goes like this: Go to AnnualCreditReport.com and choose your state. Fill out the form with your personal information. You'll have to provide your Social Security number. If that makes you nervous, that's a good thing. You should be wary of giving it out. But in this case, it's OK.

Then, you'll encounter a security test—a short multiple-choice quiz involving your credit history. It might ask which bank holds your mortgage or ask you to identify a previous address. After that, skip advertisements for getting your credit score. View your report and print it. Or, save the report to a file on your computer.

Getting reports online is easiest. But you can do it by phone by calling 1-877-322-8228 or print an online form, fill it out, and mail it to: Annual Credit Report Request Service, P.O. Box 105281, Atlanta, GA, 30348-5281.

Reading the Report

The report might appear intimidating at first, but read your way through it. After a while, it will seem like an episode of the 1950s TV series *This Is Your Life*, a diary of where you've been financially. It will have long-ago addresses, loans for cars you forgot about, department store charge cards you barely remember, and, maybe, late payments from a rough patch you went through years ago.

Don't be surprised that the bureaus have slightly different credit information in their reports. Some creditors don't report to all three bureaus.

Dispute Mistakes

If you find serious mistakes that will affect your credit-worthiness, such as credit accounts that aren't yours and incorrect negative information, follow the online instructions on how to dispute them.

If you see accurate negative information that is more than seven years old, you can dispute that too because negative information is supposed to expire off the report in that time. Bankruptcy is an exception. It can stay on credit reports for 10 years.

Don't worry too much about minor inaccuracies, such as typos or misspellings in former addresses. They don't figure into your credit score.

2. Get Your Credit Scores (Optional)

The only scores you need to worry about are your three FICO scores, which grade you on a scale of 300 to 850. Higher is better.

Others scores, some being sold by credit bureaus, are fake scores of dubious value. Some experts derisively call them FAKO scores. If the score you're retrieving doesn't specifically say it's a FICO score, it's probably not. Most lenders don't use anything but FICO-based scores. Alternative scores to FICO might become the standard in the future. But for now, FICO is all that really matters because the company that sells that score, Fair Isaac, has a virtual monopoly.

For routine monitoring, accessing your credit scores is optional. That's because scores are just based on what's in the report, and reports are free. Meanwhile, you'll probably have to pay for FICO credit scores.

But if you want or need scores, the easiest way to get them is to go online to MyFico.com and pay to view them. Two FICO scores are available, from Equifax and TransUnion. The third credit bureau, Experian, discontinued public access to its FICO credit score in early 2009. At the time of this writing, consumers no longer had access to their Experian FICO score. But they can still get their Experian credit report.

Remember, scores change all the time. You're just seeing a snapshot of your credit rating at that moment.

It's like an outdoor thermometer reading that changes from day to day. Unless something unusual happens, like a heat wave or snowstorm, the temperature reading will fluctuate within a relatively narrow range. Similarly, you won't have the exact same score every day because you're constantly using your credit, which affects the information being fed into the credit-scoring formulas. Unless something unusual happens, such as a late payment or bankruptcy, your credit score will fluctuate within a relatively narrow range.

If you've already seen your credit reports and the information is redundant, your scores will be similar. In that case, you can just retrieve one score because the others are likely to be similar.

Before you pay for scores at MyFico.com, do a quick search-engine query with the keywords "myfico.com" and "coupon code." You might find a discount code to get 10 percent to 20 percent off your order at MyFico.com.

If you don't want to pay for scores, you can get a general idea about your credit rating for free. Granted these are FAKO scores, but they can give you an idea of where you stand. Visit such Web sites as Quizzle.com, CreditKarma.com, Credit.com, and Bankrate.com. These sites offer free non-FICO scores and score simulators.

Get a CLUE: Your Insurance Report

Did you know you also have the right to get an insurance report about yourself? It's what insurers will look at when deciding whether they want to insure you. It details your claims history for home and auto insurance. In other words, it notes the instances when you've filed a claim to get money from an insurer. It's called a CLUE report. The acronym stands for Comprehensive Loss Underwriting Exchange.

You're entitled to a free report once a year. Go to www.choicetrust.com and sign up to see your claim history. If you haven't filed claims in the past five years, you might not have a CLUE report. If you have filed claims, you might have two reports, one for home insurance and one for auto insurance. Be sure to request both.

Of course, you want to check for errors in your report that could result in being rejected for insurance or paying higher premiums than necessary.

For more information, see Fact Sheet 26 at the Privacy Rights Clearinghouse, found at www.privacyrights.org.

3. Improve Your Scores

To spend smarter, which means getting the best deals and lower borrowing rates, you will have to raise your FICO scores into the 700s and ideally, beyond 750.

It helps to know what goes into a FICO score. The exact formula for calculating FICO credit scores is a secret, but we know that the biggest factor is your payment history. Paying your bills and loans on time affects 35 percent of your credit score. The amounts you owe account for 30 percent. The length of your credit history is 15 percent. Applying for new credit counts for 10 percent, as does the different types of credit you have. See Figure 6.3.

FICO Score Breakdown

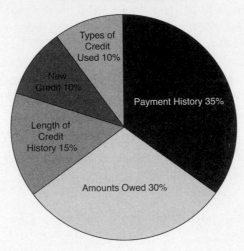

Source: MyFico.com

FIGURE 6.3   *Paying your bills on time is the most important component of your credit score.*

Notice that your FICO score only includes the credit lines you have open and how you use them. If you're a cash-paying billionaire, you probably don't have good credit scores. Your maid and gardener might have better scores.

The following sections discuss ways to improve your scores.

Fix Mistakes

Because credit scores are based on credit reports, make sure your reports don't contain inaccurate negative information.

This is a good place to talk about so-called "credit repair," as you might have heard advertised. There's no way to really repair your credit other than to correct mistakes. And you don't need to pay a company to do that for you. Disputing incorrect negative information is free and, in most cases, easy. As we talked about, dispute mistakes while accessing your reports for free once a year at AnnualCreditReport.com. Some credit repair companies will dispute all the negatives on your report, hoping creditors won't respond in the required 30 days. If creditors don't respond within 30 days to confirm that the information is correct, the negatives will be temporarily removed from your reports, raising your credit score. Of course, if a creditor responds after 30 days, the negative mark goes back onto your report.

Creditors and credit bureaus are wise to this strategy, so filing batches of disputes won't necessarily work. If you want to use this ethically questionable tactic of disputing any bad mentions on your reports, at least do it yourself rather than paying a credit-repair service.

Pay Bills

Paying your bills on time, every time, won't raise your score, but it will keep it from dropping. View due dates on bills as critical, and aim to pay a few days early. Remember, it doesn't matter if your bill somehow got lost in the mail—you still owe the money on time.

And think twice about taking a hard-line stand in a dispute with a creditor. Of course, you shouldn't allow companies to treat you unfairly, but protesting what you view as an unjust $39 charge by refusing to pay could ding up your credit report for the next seven years. Once the black mark is on your report, it could stay there for the full seven years, even if you give up and pay the bill.

Sometimes it's better to pick your battles and choose some to lose.

Find Your Ratio

Besides correcting mistakes and paying bills on time, the best thing you can do for your credit rating is to continually use credit but use very little of your available limit.

If you have several credit cards that have a combined $5,000 limit, carrying a combined balance of $4,000 is hurting your score. That's because you have an 80 percent "utilization ratio." Calculate your ratio by dividing your combined balances by your combined limit.

$$\text{Credit ratio} = \frac{\underline{\text{Combined credit balances}}}{\text{Combined credit limits}}$$

Aim to get that ratio down to the 30 percent range. To optimize your score, aim for less than 10 percent. Remember, you score doesn't care whether you pay off the balance, only how much of your available credit limit you're using at any given time. If you're always at zero percent, meaning you don't use the cards at all, the cards won't contribute to your credit score after a while.

Improve Your Ratio

Paying off debt so you're carrying smaller balances will help your ratio—and your overall financial health. Carrying balances does not help your scores.

And don't close accounts. Keep open your old or unwanted accounts, even if you paid them off and don't use them. The more available and unused credit, the better for your score. Besides helping your ratio, the old accounts help to increase the average age of your credit lines. Remember that your length of credit history is a significant factor in the FICO score.

One exception: If you know that you will spend more on unnecessary purchases just because you have the available credit, close the accounts. You'll do more damage to your overall financial health than the relatively minor improvement to your credit score.

Cautiously raise credit limits. It helps to have a lot of available credit to help your ratio. But opening a lot of new credit accounts at once will likely hurt your credit score in the short term. A strategy to help your score without hurting it would be to regularly ask your current credit card company to raise your current limit "without pulling a credit report." Applying for new credit cards is problematic because you have to use those new cards a little to show them as active accounts, but not use them so much it hurts your ratio. All that assumes you can have open accounts and not use them irresponsibly by charging things you can't afford.

You can also improve your ratio by double-paying your credit card bill, by making two credit-card payments a month. This artificially lowers your balance reported to credit bureaus. Make a payment in the middle of your billing cycle, which will lower the amount the creditor reports to the credit bureau on the statement closing date.

WARNING

Be sure to make the second payment after the closing date and before the due date, so you aren't socked with a late payment, says Liz Pulliam Weston, author of Your Credit Score. *Some billing systems need to see a payment made between the statement closing date and the due date to register you as paid on time, even if you made more than the minimum payment earlier in the month.*

Type "A" personalities, take note: Forget perfect. If your FICO score is 780 or above, don't bother trying to improve it. Lenders already view you as perfect. You gain very little—and potentially nothing at all—by succumbing to a perfectionist personality and trying to improve your score to 800 and above. In fact, many actions you take might end up hurting your score. Just keep on doing what you've been doing.

Establishing Credit

Establishing credit, or reestablishing healthy credit after a bankruptcy, can be a challenge.

- Establish credit. If you're new to credit or recovering from a bankruptcy, you might have to apply for a secured credit card, which requires you to pay money into an account and then draw on it with the credit card. Make sure it converts to a regular credit card after a reasonable period of time, for example,

18 months. You can also apply for installment loans, such as an auto loan, which will help build credit by adding a different type of loan. The problem is, without a high credit score, you'll pay a high interest rate. And if, because of that high rate you default on the loan, you're back to having terrible credit.

- A note on credit for college students. Oddly, college students, with or without jobs, can get credit easily by getting a credit card. Applications literally litter college campuses. Credit card companies have learned that when college students can't pay their credit card bills, mommy and daddy usually step in and pay. That makes students a pretty good credit risk. Whether your college student *should* have a credit card is a different matter. A college student can apply for a card without a parent's approval. So, have a conversation before the first trip to campus about whether your child should get a card.

How You Pay

Spending smart isn't just about what you buy, but how you pay.

The ultraorganized and responsible consumer might gain advantages by using mostly credit cards, while those struggling with money management should stick with mostly cash. For those in between, the decision lies in the details—although, everybody should be writing as few personal checks as possible.

One reasonable strategy for consumers who fall between the ultradisciplined and financially challenged is to use cash and debit cards for everyday purchases. Then use credit cards for big-ticket purchases and online transactions to ensure you get the added consumer protections credit cards provide.

Noncredit Payment Methods

Setting aside credit cards for a moment, here is a good preference for cash payment methods.

Noncredit Payment Methods, 1-2-3

1. **Consider cash as king.**
2. **Do debit right.**
3. **Limit use of checks.**

1. Consider Cash as King

Paying with cash has a few drawbacks. For example, it might not be convenient to pay for very expensive items with paper bills and coins. You'll get no rewards points or fringe benefits when paying with cash. If you haven't chosen a bank wisely, you might have to pay ATM withdrawal fees. You receive no automatic record of spending like you get with credit card bills, canceled checks, and bank statements. And, of course, there's the some-what remote possibility you'll be mugged and lose your cash that way.

But using cash can be a fabulous idea. For one, it could help you curb impulse spending. Studies show that consumers spend about 20 percent more when using plastic, rather than cash. That's because people suffer a psychological pain when handing over bills and coins. It feels much more real than swiping plastic. That's because the transfer of funds is right in front of you, rather than occurring in some invisible transfer of electrons among banks. The transfer is proximate enough to feel the loss.

Just as important, cash never has finance charges or overdraft fees or many of the negatives of paying with plastic.

A related and profound point is this: When you use cash, you can spend the money you have but no more. If you don't have the money, you can't buy it. You must stop consuming when the money runs out. If you have $200 in cash to spend at the supermarket, you could be forced to place items back on the shelf if you don't have enough money.

Surely, these points are not news to you, but you might not have thought about them in a long time. For these reasons, cash is still a great form of currency.

QUICK TIP

Nowadays you can actually withdraw more money from an ATM than you have in your account. Banks call it "courtesy overdraft protection." They give you more money than you have in your account and then slap you with an overdraft fee of $20 to $40 and impose high interest charges on the money they have advanced. This also is offered for overdrawing your account by personal check or debit card. To avoid overdraft fees and interest charges, keep track of spending and obtain real overdraft protection, where you instruct the bank to dip into another account, such as savings, when a checking account is over-drawn. And keep a cushion of about $500 in your account at all times.

---

2. Do Debit Right

In general, using debit cards is a fine alternative to using cash and credit cards. Also known as a check card, a debit card is more convenient than cash or personal checks. You use it like a credit card, but the money comes immediately out of your bank account. Most double as an ATM card to make cash withdrawals. They also provide a record of spending and avoid the risk of finance charges. Some debit cards provide rewards.

The big drawback of debit cards is they are not afforded the same fraud protections under federal law as credit cards. With a stolen credit card, you can lose no more than $50 out of pocket. That's federal law. But federal law is weaker when it comes to debit cards. With a debit card, you must report it within two business days to receive the $50 liability limit. Otherwise, you're on the hook for $500, or after 60 days you could lose everything a thief steals from your bank account.

Individual card companies, such as Visa and MasterCard, have policies that promise to limit your debit-card liability to zero, but these policies are not as strong as federal law and could change. And even if the bank eventually puts money back in your account—and it doesn't have to for at least two weeks—you could struggle to pay bills while you and the bank sort out the mess.

You'll have to decide for yourself whether less fraud protection under federal law is a reason to avoid carrying debit cards in lieu of credit cards. If you don't want the direct-debit feature of your card, you can ask your bank to replace your debit card with an ATM-only card, so you still have ATM access to cash.

Another drawback of debit cards arises from merchant *blocking*. Blocking is when a merchant, at a gas station or hotel, for example, routinely withholds an amount on a debit card until the transaction is fully processed. That blocked amount is temporarily unavailable, meaning you could overdraw your account if you don't have an adequate cushion. That can result in overdraft fees.

And debit cards don't help your creditworthiness, like credit cards do. For these reasons, the Privacy Rights Clearinghouse, a privacy advocacy group, recommends consumers never use, or even carry, debit cards.

That's a hard-line stance against a potentially useful money tool. Even considering all the potential negatives about debit cards, I like them as a cash alternative for people who have trouble handling credit cards responsibly.

QUICK TIP

When using a debit card, choose to provide a signature rather than PIN—choose "credit" rather than "debit"—if your bank charges for PIN transactions or grants rewards points only for signature transactions. Either method subtracts money directly from your bank account.

---

3. Limit Use of Checks

In short, checks are a lousy form of currency.

It's true that you won't incur finance charges with checks, like you might with credit cards. And you can track spending in the checkbook register. But the advantages mostly stop there.

Checks are the most inconvenient form of payment because it takes time to fill out a check, you have to pay for and reorder blank checks, and some merchants don't accept them. Any "float" time you receive between writing the check and money being taken from your account has shrunk dramatically with electronic processing of checks.

More problematic is that checks are at the most risk for fraud and identity theft. Most everything a thief would need to steal your identity is on your check, including your name, address, and bank account number.

So, regularly paying bills by check just isn't a good idea anymore.

One of the few occasions when checks are more convenient than other payment methods is when you're paying another individual and don't want to use cash— if you're paying back your sister for splitting the cost of dad's birthday gift, for example. If you are mailing checks, be very wary of putting a check in your mailbox for outgoing mail. Again, a thief only needs to pluck it out of the box.

QUICK TIP

Check washing is a scam in which a thief steals a check and chemically erases—or washes—the payee and amount, fills in new payment information for himself, and cleans out your bank account. You can avoid check washing by using special pens, such as the Uni-ball 207 gel pen, which retails for about $2. Its ink cannot be chemically erased.

Layaway and No-No-No Sales

The hallmark of a bad way to pay is one that allows or entices you to buy stuff you cannot afford. By "afford," I mean having money to pay for it *before* you make the purchase. Timing is crucial. The right way is: money first, then buy. That's as opposed to the typical way: Buy first, and then figure out how to pay later.

That's the biggest reason to avoid layaway and sales featuring "no down payment, no interest, no payments."

- **Layaway.** Layaway isn't evil. It's just illogical and unnecessary.

  Layaway is when you select items you want to buy, take them to a special layaway department, and place a down payment on the purchases, usually with an additional service fee of $5 or $10. You leave items at the retailer and periodically return to make payments on the items. When they're paid off, you take them home.

  Some shoppers are fierce supporters of layaway. A segment of customers were furious at Wal-Mart in 2006, when it discontinued its layaway program.

  Layaway can be useful for nabbing hard-to-get items, such as a hot-selling toy while it's in stock and locking in a sale price that won't be available later when you have the cash. A potential third reason comes during the holidays when you need to hide gifts from nosy children. You can leave them in the layaway department at a store rather than risk discovery in your home.

But for any other reason, layaway is among the worst of purchasing scenarios—the retailer has your money and the merchandise. You leave the store with nothing. If you fail to finish making your payments, you don't get the goods and you often incur an additional fee.

A predominant attitude among layaway lovers is that it's a better idea than paying by credit card and incurring interest charges. But that's based on a false premise because it disregards two better choices: saving the money first or not buying it at all.

Instead of making payments on your layaway merchandise, what if you shoved cash for those payments under a mattress or into a cookie jar? The outcome would be the same. You return to the store when you have enough money and buy it. It takes no more time—you get the merchandise just as quickly—and you avoid the layaway fee. If you have the discipline to use layaway, you should certainly have the discipline to stash away some cash, which takes less effort.

And in some cases, layaway is mathematically worse than charging on a credit card. Imagine you pay a $5 fee for a 30-day layaway on a $100 purchase. If you instead used a credit card with an annual interest rate of 18 percent, it would charge 1.5 percent for that same 30-day period, or $1.50. In that scenario, layaway costs three times more.

- **No-no-no sales.** Take a hint from the name, and consider these a no-no. "No down payment, no interest, no payments for 12 months" sales usually feature a fine-print gotcha. In some cases, the slightest slip-up in payment, such as missing a payment or not paying the balance by the end of the promotional period, means you'll be back-charged exorbitant interest from the date of purchase. In addition, many no-no-no sales require you to apply for a store's charge card, which is likely to lower your credit score, at least temporarily.

Granted, diligent and savvy consumers can use no-no-no sales to their advantage by earning bank interest on their money for the duration of the no-payments period. But why? The interest you'll earn is miniscule and the penalty for a minor mistake is harsh.

Don't outfox yourself. When you buy something, pay for it.

Credit Cards

"Guns don't kill people, people kill people,
and monkeys do too—if they have a gun."

—Comedian Eddie Izzard

A credit card is like a loaded handgun. It's not the tool that makes it good or bad. It's the user. That's why credit cards, as a payment method, deserve their own section in this book. They can be a convenient and even lucrative form of payment, or they can be disastrous. They are, at once, good and evil.

Maybe the single-biggest advantage to credit cards is being able to use somebody else's money—that of the bank issuing the card. Think about it. When paying with cash, checks, and debit cards, you're putting your money at risk in the transaction. With credit cards, you put the bank's money at risk. You can dispute a charge and the bank has to fight with the vendor. Meanwhile, you don't pay. If a card is stolen, you just report it. Your cash is not vulnerable.

Used well, the credit card is the only form of payment that builds your credit history so you can obtain lower rates on other products such as auto loans and insurance. Credit cards also provide rewards, such as cash, airline miles, or merchandise points. Some offer extended warranties on products purchased with the card and other perks that vary among cards.

At the same time, credit cards carry the biggest downsides of any payment method. Namely, consumers frequently spend more when they charge purchases, as we said previously, and many incur outrageous finance charges that sometimes top 30 percent. Late-payment and over-the-limit fees are also punitive. Those disadvantages, if they apply to you, dwarf any advantages of credit cards.

If you are philosophically opposed to credit cards, I have no problem with that. Don't use them. Just realize you're forgoing some convenience, consumer protections, and rewards that credit cards provide. But if you spend less as a result of using cash only, you could be adequately compensated for your philosophical stand.

Here's how to get the most out of your credit cards.

Credit Cards, 1-2-3

1. **Never carry a balance.**
2. **Know your perks.**
3. **Maintain your card.**

1. Never Carry a Balance

Never is a strong word. But carrying balances on credit cards from month to month is so destructive to your finances that it's worth using strong language.

For those who carry a credit card balance from month to month, credit cards can be downright evil. Interest rates can easily top 20 percent and push toward 30 percent, which is outrageous. You could be in big money trouble if you're paying only the minimum payment each month. It's wildly expensive. See Figure 6.4.

What if you made only the minimum payment of $200 on a balance of $8,000?

Credit card balance: $8,000

Interest rate: 18%

Minimum payment: $200

Years to pay off: 30

Interest paid: $11,615.

FIGURE 6.4 *Minimum payment predicament*

So, paying high interest on credit cards, if you can possibly avoid it, is foolish. If you regularly carry balances, you have already figured that out.

Yet, nearly half of American households carry a balance from month to month, according to the Federal Reserve. You can view this statistic a couple of different ways. First, it's shameful that almost half of American households are borrowing money on their credit cards, with many paying outrageous interest rates. That's even truer if much of the balance includes dinners out, unnecessary electronic gadgets, and other highly optional charges.

The second way to look at the statistic is that half of Americans carry no balance at all. So, if you justify having a balance "because everybody does," it just ain't so.

Also, don't take comfort in reports that say the average balance on credit cards is $10,000. MSN Money columnist Liz Pulliam Weston is the foremost crusader against this so-called fact, which originates from CardWeb.com. It has been reported by the media literally hundreds of times in recent years. CardWeb.com reported that in 2007 outstanding credit card debt was $9,840 per household. Weston points out that the number only includes households that have a credit card, which eliminates from the average all those households with zero balances because they don't have cards. The stat also includes business credit cards, which can have huge balances, especially with business travel. What business credit card balances have to do with household debt, I have no idea. Just as important, it reports the total balance as a snapshot, regardless of how many of those people paid off the balance before incurring finance charges.

The point is, not everybody is carrying credit card balances, and you shouldn't either.

As I alluded to earlier, part of the reason people run balances on credit cards is because credit cards don't seem like real money. Handing over plastic to a cashier doesn't stimulate the same emotional pain as handing over a fistful of twenty-dollar bills. Indeed, studies have shown that consumers spend more with credit cards than cash, which explains the growing presence of card readers at every retail cash register. Retailers want you to overspend.

So, even people who pay off balances every month could be overspending just by virtue of the payment method they're using.

2. Know Your Perks

Despite all those negatives, credit cards have advantages—for "deadbeats." You would think credit card "deadbeats" is a term for people who don't pay their bills. But, in fact, deadbeats are what credit card companies call customers who pay off their balances each month. These customers don't pay the issuer any interest or fees. In essence, they give themselves a free ride by enjoying all the advantages of credit cards and suffering none of the downsides. Don't feel too sorry for credit card companies, though. They still make money from the merchants you buy from.

Being a credit-card deadbeat is a good thing.

One of the advantages of credit cards is they help establish and maintain your credit rating, which translates to real money. You can get less-expensive mortgages and car loans when you have a better credit rating. And you might even get cheaper auto insurance, as some insurers now use credit ratings in determining your premiums.

Another huge benefit is putting the credit card company between the merchant and your cash. That's why it's best to use a credit card for online and mail-order purchases in case a dispute arises.

Cards have many fringe benefits too. Most people overlook these perks. They include purchase protection, extended warranties, merchandise discounts, travel insurance, rental car insurance, price protection, lost luggage help, favorable exchange rates on foreign currencies, and others.

I won't go into details about these offerings because they vary by card. But make a note on your to-do list to investigate all the perks of credit cards you carry in your wallet. You can read about the benefits online at the card-issuer's Web site or call the phone number on the back of your card and ask, "What are my card perks?"

QUICK TIP

Merchants can't require a minimum purchase for using a Visa or MasterCard credit card. A provision in their agreements with card companies requires them to accept charges of any amount. Of course, there's not much you can do about a merchant refusing to make a small sale, except report them to the credit card company.

---

3. Maintain Your Card

Maintaining your card doesn't mean keeping the card free of fingerprints or making sure the signature on the back is legible. It means continually negotiating better terms on your credit card account.

One secret of the credit card industry is this: As bad as card issuers sometimes treat their customers, they hate to lose them.

It's very expensive to acquire new customers. So, threatening to stop using the card—or better yet threatening to transfer your balances to another card—can be effective with customer service representatives on the phone.

The point is you have leverage. And you should use it at least annually to improve the terms of your deal with the bank issuing the card. This remained true, even after the credit crunch that began in 2008.

The first thing to do is ask your card issuer for a better interest rate, even if you don't carry a balance. That's because, for better or worse, credit cards are a short-term source of funds. You never know when you might have to break the cardinal rule of "never carry a balance."

Call the number on the back of the card, and just ask. If you're unsatisfied with the answer, ask for a supervisor. Still not satisfied? Call back in a few weeks and do it again. The better payment history you have, the more likely you'll succeed.

The next thing to do is call back and ask for a higher credit limit. This is a tactic discussed earlier about how to improve your credit score. Be sure to ask, "How much can you raise my limit, *without pulling my credit report*?" That's because an official inquiry into your credit report could temporarily lower your credit score. You're looking for something for nothing here. The point of raising your limit is to improve your credit score by lowering your ratio of credit used to your credit limit. A secondary reason for raising your limit is to avoid over-the-limit penalty fees, if you're the type of person who nearly maxes out your credit cards.

> ### QUICK TIP
>
> *Speaking of maxing out, if you're at the video store wondering which blockbuster to rent next, head over to the documentary aisle and check out the 2007 movie, Maxed Out. It's a disturbing and enlightening exposé on how credit card companies prey on the weak in society. In fact, their profits depend on it.*

The final thing to ask your credit card company is for fees to be waived, even if it's your fault. If the card company hits you with a $40 late-payment fee or over-the-limit fee, call up and just ask for them to waive it. If you're a good customer and it's your first slip-up, they will almost certainly waive the fee. It's worth a phone call.

How to Choose a Rewards Credit Card

In choosing any credit card, the primary question is: Will you carry a balance? If so, get the lowest interest rate you can and pay off the balance. Forget rewards cards, which typically have higher interest rates.

But if you're what the industry calls a deadbeat, meaning you pay your credit card bill in full every month, you probably want a rewards card.

How to Choose a Rewards Credit Card, 1-2-3

1. Go online.
2. Choose cash back.
3. Get more than 1 percent.

A rewards card gives you something back based on your purchases. Some give frequent flyer airline miles, some merchandise points, others cash. Some give you greater rewards based on where you shop, boosting rewards at gas stations and supermarkets, for example.

There's something so alluring about getting something for nothing. Assuming you have a high enough credit score to qualify for rewards cards, here's how to choose.

1. Go Online

A number of Web sites will help you choose a rewards card, or, at least, you can survey the choices. Among the Web sites are CardRatings.com, IndexCreditCards.com, and LowCards.com. The previously mentioned BillShrink.com is also worth using. And, watch your mailbox. Some card deals are only offered directly by mail to certain potential customers. And check with your credit union. If you don't have a credit union, you probably qualify to join one. See www.findacreditunion.com.

2. Choose Cash Back

Although you can choose among a wide range of credit card rewards, choose one with cash back on all your purchases. The problem with points and airline miles is the card issuer can change the value of those "currencies" anytime it wants. It can require more points for the same merchandise or more miles for the same airline ticket. Never mind the hassle of trying to cash in points or miles—fat chance you'll be able to use those frequent-flyer miles during a holiday, for example. Frequent-flyer miles can expire, and many miles cards will charge you an annual fee, which cuts into whatever benefit you get.

Curtis E. Arnold, author of *How You Can Profit from Credit Cards*, points out that it could take three years to earn a free ticket purchased with frequent-flyer miles from your card, assuming annual spending of $8,000. If that card carries an $80 per year annual fee, your "free" ticket just cost you $240 in fees, compared with the many no-fee credit cards available. At the same level of spending, you might have earned enough with a simple 1 percent–back cash rewards card to pay for a ticket.

QUICK TIP

If you already have airline miles, use them soon. With a struggling airline industry, airline miles will probably become less valuable. Airlines are charging larger fees for cashing in frequent-flyer miles for supposedly "free" flights. And airlines are cutting flights, which might make it harder to use miles. Experts also believe major carriers will start requiring flyers to use more points for flights.

The card issuer can't change the value of cash. Moreover, guess what you can buy with cash?

Anything, including merchandise and airline tickets.

So, cash is a far superior currency than points and miles because it gives you more options. And cash programs are also easier to use. The real dollar value of points or airline miles should have to be far higher than cash to persuade you to voluntarily lose the flexibility of cash and accept an inferior form of rewards payment.

Be wary of charity rewards credit cards, too. The good part about a card that donates your rebate to a charity is it makes your contributions automatic. The bad part is most cards donate just 1 percent of your spending or less to the charity. A better plan is to use a cash-back card and write an annual check to the charity for the amount of your yearly rebate. The charity will get more, and you can take a tax deduction.

Once you get a cash-back rewards credit card, throw as many charges on it as you can. Even middle-income households are likely to get back several hundred dollars a year, with big spenders getting back more than $1,000.

3. Get More Than 1 Percent

You can do better than a cash rebate of 1 percent on all your purchases. Many cards offer 2 percent to 5 percent on certain types of purchases, such as gasoline and groceries, and 1 percent on everything else.

As of this writing, a great card for big spenders— charging well over $1,000 a month—is the American Express Blue Cash card. With a tiered reward system, bigger cash rebates kick in after charging $6,500. Details are at AmericanExpress.com.

There's no clear choice for smaller spenders. Find a card that gives you at least 1 percent right away, gives you the most rewards for your spending patterns, and will cut a check or credit your account at $25 or $50 increments.

Offers for rewards cards change regularly.

Besides getting more than 1 percent back, here are other considerations:

- Avoid cards that charge an annual fee.
- Give preference to cards that automatically send you the rewards payment as a check or credit the amount to your account. That's better than having to remember to request a check when your points accumulate to a certain cash-out level.
- Choose a program with no rewards limit, or at least one you're not likely to max out.
- Look for a bonus reward for signing up.
- If you choose an American Express or Discover card as your primary card, you'll need a rewards Visa or MasterCard backup because they are accepted in more places.

One final warning: Don't get so infatuated with rewards that you end up spending more than you would otherwise just to earn more rewards. It's likely to be a net loss for you.

How to Get Out of Debt

Here's a newsflash: The first step to getting out of debt is to stop adding to it. You do that by saying "no" to a series of payments with interest and, instead, paying in full.

The TV show *Saturday Night Live* a few years ago aired a skit with comedian Steve Martin, who was guest-hosting. It was a spoof on an infomercial promoting a revolutionary get-out-of debt plan. The "unique program" was titled, "Don't buy stuff you cannot afford."

The skit opened with a discouraged couple sitting at their kitchen table wondering how they'll ever get out of debt. Enter the author of a one-page book, *Don't Buy Stuff You Cannot Afford*.

Woman reads aloud from the book: "If you do not have any money, you should not buy anything."

Woman to husband: "There's a whole section here on buying expensive things using money you save."

Couple looks thoroughly confused.

Woman: "What if I want something but I don't have any money?"

Author: "You don't buy it!"

Man: "Let's say I don't have enough money to buy something. Should I buy it anyway?"

Author: "No!"

Woman: "What if you have the money, can you buy something?"

Author: "Yes!"

This skit goes on, but you get the idea. The spoof infomercial says if you order now you can receive the additional book, *Seriously, If You Don't Have the Money, Don't Buy it*, along with a 12-month subscription to *Stop Buying Stuff* magazine.

The point is to stop the buying and borrowing behavior that got you into debt in the first place.

How to Get Out of Debt, 1-2-3

1. **Quit borrowing money.**
2. **Quit saving money.**
3. **Pay small debts first.**

1. Quit Borrowing Money

If your debt is growing, there are only two explanations. You're spending too much money, which this book should be able to help with. Or, you have an income problem. You're charging necessities on the card because you don't make enough money to cover bare living expenses. Figuring out the reason for running up credit card debt is the first step toward making sure it doesn't happen again.

The culprit of debt is often credit cards. If you can't trust yourself with credit cards, stop using them—cut them up, freeze them in a block of ice in your freezer, whatever. Just don't close accounts because that will hurt your credit score.

Well-meaning people will advise you to transfer balances to lower-rate cards or continually surf the balance from low introductory rate to low introductory rate. Card surfing is not inherently bad, but it's not nearly as effective as actually paying down the card balances. Surfing merely shuffles debt around. And you might even add to debt by incurring transfer fees.

For people in deep debt, it's like the old metaphor of rearranging deck chairs on the Titanic. It doesn't address that sinking feeling.

So, unless you have a credit card at more than 20 percent interest and can get a substantially lower rate, focus your energy on paying more and surfing less.

This is one case where "throwing money at the problem" actually works.

2. Quit Saving Money

This might be surprising advice. After all, saving money is a good thing, right?

The problem is your debts are probably costing you more than your savings are earning for you. For example, you might be paying 18 percent interest on your credit card debt and earning less than 5 percent on savings. That's a huge net loss.

In a simple-interest example, depositing $5,000 in a 5 percent savings account earns you $250 a year, which the government then taxes. But if you used that $5,000 to pay down an 18 percent-interest credit card, you save $900. And you pay no tax on that kind of savings.

In fact, after you have a starter emergency fund of $2,500, you can use other saved money to pay off high-interest debt. Again, it makes no sense to have a certificate of deposit earning 5 or 6 percent while paying double-digit interest on debt.

A possible exception to the "Quit Saving" rule is if you have an automatic retirement savings plan, such as a 401(k), 403(b), or automatic deposits to a Roth IRA. If that kind of plan is already on autopilot with 10 percent or less of your income, you can leave it alone. A definite exception is if your employer matches your contributions in a retirement plan. You want to capture all of that free money you can.

However, if you can get intense about paying off your debt, stopping retirement savings for a short time will get you out of debt faster.

3. Pay Small Debts First

How do you prioritize which debts to pay extra on? The biggest debt or smallest debt? Highest interest rate or lowest?

I like a hybrid plan that goes like this:

- Pay off debts of less than $1,000 first, from smallest to largest, while paying minimums on other debts.
- Then, pay off debts greater than $1,000 from highest interest rate to lowest, while paying minimums on others.

Each time you kill off a debt, you apply that payment to the next debt. When that's done, you roll the combined total into the next debt, and so on. That's the debt snowball.

This debt-repayment plan is a modified version of a plan espoused by Dave Ramsey, a radio-show host and author of *The Total Money Makeover*. He didn't invent the idea of paying debts smallest to largest and snow-balling them, but he's best known for it.

Of course, mathematics says you should pay the highest interest-rate debts first to avoid paying the most interest. This is easy to understand and logical.

But getting out of debt is a lot like dieting. It's difficult and takes a huge helping of self-discipline. By paying off small debts first, you can wipe out a number of them and feel like you're gaining traction and succeeding. It's the atta-boy or atta-girl to help you keep going and pay off more debt, just like losing a few pounds during the first days of a diet. It gives you encouragement to continue.

So much with money has more to do with what's between our ears than what's in our wallets. The emotional lift from wiping out small debts is well worth whatever small amount of interest you might have saved by paying first on a huge high-interest debt that takes years to eliminate. Just make sure to get rid of those small debts quickly.

Once you get to your large debts, you'll be better off paying more attention to the interest rate. For example, you would pay off a $10,000 credit-card balance at 18 percent before paying off a $9,000 auto loan at 7 percent.

Here are answers to some other common debt questions.

What about My Mortgage?

Your mortgage, especially if it's at a favorable fixed rate, is the one debt you can relax about. It comes far down the priority list. You don't need to pay it off early until you have your other financial goals achieved, especially retirement savings.

The reason is you're probably paying a relatively low interest rate. If you can take a mortgage-interest deduction on your income taxes, your interest rate is effectively even lower.

I'm not saying never pay your mortgage off early. Just have retirement planning, kids' college savings, and other essential financial goals well under way first.

Should I Use a Home Equity Loan to "Pay Off" My Credit Card Debt?

The good news is you can get a lower interest rate by using the stored value in your house to pay debt. But this debt swap can be dangerous for a couple of reasons.

First, you must realize you're not "paying off" anything. You're just moving your debt. If moving your debt makes you feel better, that might be a bad thing. That's because you haven't addressed the fundamental problem: spending more money than you could afford. To solve a debt problem long-term, you'll have to dig into that question. Either your income is too low or your spending is too high.

Second, you're moving unsecured debt to secured debt. In English, that means if you don't pay your credit card bill, the bank can't do much to you, except to bug you with phone calls and damage your credit score. If you don't pay a home-equity loan, on the other hand, the bank can take your house. I think losing your house is a bigger deal.

So, if there's any chance you won't be able to pay, keep the debt on credit cards. If you discovered the reason you're in debt and have permanently addressed the problem, shifting to a lower interest rate with a home equity loan will probably save money.

Is Credit Counseling Worthwhile?

Credit counseling can be a good idea or a bad one. But it's a more complicated decision than you might think.

Often, you will pay money for the service, and your creditworthiness might be trashed in the process. Though these agencies might be technically nonprofits, it doesn't mean they are charities offering free or even legitimate assistance. You could end up paying high fees and getting bad advice. In fact, one thing to look for is the free education and advice an agency is willing to provide. It might hint at a good counselor.

These warnings don't mean you shouldn't seek credit counseling—and if you're filing for bankruptcy, you're required to get it. But you should know that hiring a credit counselor is an important spending decision, so you should treat it like you're hiring a contractor to renovate your kitchen. That means interviewing multiple credit counselors.

First, determine whether you're a good candidate. Often a credit-counseling agency doesn't do anything you couldn't do for yourself. Evaluate all of your options before entering credit counseling, including developing a better spending and savings plan, and negotiating with creditors by yourself.

Enlisting a credit counselor will be noted on your credit report. It will damage your ability to borrow money at good interest rates because future creditors will see a notation that you are in credit counseling. However, credit counseling doesn't directly affect your three-digit credit score. Of course, many distressed people seeking counseling have already badly dinged up their creditworthiness, so an additional bad mark is only incremental.

If you feel overwhelmed, you're using credit cards for daily living expenses, and you've considered tapping your home equity or retirement plan to pay debts because you don't know what else to do, you might be a good candidate for counseling.

If you decide to go through with credit counseling, beware of an agency that says it can eliminate your debt quickly and erase your bad credit history. The agency is not reputable. The same goes for debt-settlement companies, which are not really credit counselors. Many advise you to stop paying your bills and become a true deadbeat, in hopes you can settle your debts for less than the amount owed. This tactic can work for some desperate people who have the right types of creditors, but it can be expensive, and results are not guaranteed.

You could end up owing more than before you started. Even if successful, you'll have a ruined credit score and probably owe taxes on the amount forgiven.

When you sign up with a credit counseling agency, find out how it makes money. Be dogged when asking about how the fee-structure works. Reasonable one-time fees and monthly fees are in the $25 to $75 range. If total fees are measured in hundreds or even thousands of dollars, you're in the wrong ballpark.

Many agencies will try to get you on a debt management plan, or DMP. It allows the counseling agency to work with creditors on your behalf. It often can get lower interest rates on some of your debts, get more flexible repayment schedules, and potentially get extra fees waived. You pay the agency regular lump sums, and it distributes the money to your creditors, according to the repayment plan, which often lasts three to five years. DMPs are generally for unsecured debts, such as credit card debt, not auto loans and mortgages.

But know that DMPs are how counseling agencies make most of their money. They get paid by creditors, such as banks that issue credit cards. That establishes a dicey relationship about whom the counselor works for—you or the banks. If counselors are paid on commission for setting you up with a DMP, look elsewhere for help. If a counselor is pushing a debt management plan within the first 20 minutes of learning your financial picture, you might not be dealing with a reputable agency.

A counselor's affiliation with industry groups, such as the National Foundation for Credit Counseling, found at www.nfcc.org, raises your chances of dealing with a good counselor. Many NFCC members go by the name Consumer Credit Counseling Service, or CCCS. Another certifying group is the Association for Independent Consumer Credit Counseling Agencies, found at www.aiccca.org.

PART III

Spending Smart Tomorrow

Chapter 7

How to Save Money

As I talked about in Chapter 2, "First Things First," goals give you direction and can provide peace of mind. They even have application in daily life. With all the marketing bombarding us every day and fueling our wants, a set of goals helps us to say no. They remind us there's something we want more than the tempting purchase right in front of us.

Even when you have written savings goals, it takes a lot of willpower to consciously stash away money each month. We humans are hardwired to consume immediately. So, saving for future needs and wants goes against our nature.

That's why saving toward goals must be automatic.

It could be an automatic 401(k) deduction from your paycheck to fund retirement or an automatic draft from your checking account that adds to your "snorkeling in Bahamas fund."

You put money toward priorities first, and then you're free to spend what's left on daily living. In that way, having goals is freeing. You don't have to be constantly wondering if you're doing all the right savings things and feeling guilty about indulging in small daily purchases.

You might have heard this called "Pay yourself first" because you stash away money for your goals before paying everybody else. It's also an alternative to a full-fledged household budget. By saving first, you create an artificial environment of money scarcity in the household. It erects boundaries to our spending. Specifically, it cuts down on the cash we have around, so we don't spend as much. It's based on the idea that we'll spend all that's available to us unless there's a darned good reason not to. This is why increasing your retirement contribution is relatively painless. It's true, you'll have less money to spend each week, but you unconsciously adjust your spending accordingly. Unless it's a huge jump in savings, you won't even notice the difference.

Automatic savings leads automatically to lower spending.

Erecting these artificial boundaries for money is useful. In America, we get very used to abundance and "unlimited." Do you remember when we used to pay for a certain number of hours each month for Internet access? Now, most Internet access is unlimited. We used to pay by the minute for long-distance phone calls. Today, many calling plans include unlimited long distance.

For decades, gasoline seemed unlimited because no matter how much we used, the price was always about $1.25 per gallon. Of course, it only seemed unlimited, as we found out in recent years, as demand grew and prices fluctuated wildly.

Diamonds aren't rare, and aren't intrinsically valuable. They only cost a lot because diamond companies restrict the supply and constantly advertise that diamonds are special. And somehow they became a mandatory element of marriage proposals. Producers of diamonds create an artificial environment of scarcity.

You can do the same thing with your household finances.

Of course, the big problem with the artificial scarcity plan is the availability of credit. Whether credit cards or a home-equity line of credit, that ability to borrow money easily removes the scarcity boundaries you artificially set up. It makes no sense to pay yourself first and save money earning 3 percent interest but exceed your boundaries by spending on credit cards and pay 18 or 29 percent interest. So, to use the artificial scarcity plan, you must not borrow money for consumer purchases.

It's like being on a diet and throwing away all the cookies and potato chips, creating a scarcity of junk food in the kitchen. The only thing to eat is healthful stuff, so you do. But such a diet plan is doomed if you regularly stop by the convenience store for donuts and Doritos, in effect sidestepping the scarcity boundaries you artificially set up. (In case you got lost with that analogy, credit cards are the convenience-store Doritos.)

In the end, paying yourself first is voluntary self-deception, like setting your clock ahead 10 minutes so you won't be late. If you are committed to the deception, it works great.

Short-Term Savings

Don't be shy about opening separate bank accounts for each of your short-term goals. Of course, you want accounts that won't charge you any fees. It's true that opening more accounts slightly complicates things because you have more accounts to keep track of. But it's well worth it because you'll be very clear about what your short-term spending goals are and how you're funding them. It's similar to the simple envelope system for daily spending, with one envelope containing money for food, another for clothing, and so on.

Short-Term Savings, 1-2-3

1. **Emergency fund.**
2. **Car fund.**
3. **Seasonal fund.**

If you're going to be stashing cash in separate accounts, it would be nice to earn a little interest on the money. That's why an online savings account is a great choice. For years, among the best choices for online savings accounts have been:

- EmigrantDirect.com
- INGDirect.com
- HSBCdirect.com

Frankly, it doesn't matter much which one you choose. Go with whichever account happens to be paying a higher interest rate than the others at the time you look at them. Rates change often, but historically, they have been in the same narrow range. You'll drive yourself crazy always trying to get the absolute highest interest rate. Remember the concept of "good enough?" Deposits at all three banks are insured by the Federal Deposit Insurance Corp. (FDIC), up to $100,000[1] per depositor. And they are all good enough.

Opening an online account is fairly easy. Follow instructions on the Web sites, and fill out forms. You will have to electronically link a personal checking account to the savings account to make automatic deposits. You will also have to provide your Social Security number.

1. Emergency Fund

Whether you call it a rainy-day fund, an emergency fund, or a cash cushion, having cash available for when bad things happen is fundamental to financial planning.

What exactly constitutes an emergency fund? The typical advice is also the most conservative definition: cash equal to three to six months of living expenses. I would modify that to be three to six months of "barebones" expenses, meaning enough money to pay rent or mortgage, food, utilities, transportation, insurance, and so on.

Why? Because in a financial crisis—think, losing your job—you should immediately cut back on nonessential spending—no going out to eat, no clothing purchases, and no golfing. You could even start canceling your gym membership, your cable TV service, and your fancy hairdresser appointment. The point is you need a cushion to pay for necessary expenses, a total far less than expenses during flush times.

How do you decide on whether to save three months of expenses or six? It depends on your circumstances. For example, two-income families have less of a need for a large emergency fund, especially if both earners make about the same amount of money. That's because a job loss, among the most serious of emergencies, doesn't wipe out the entire household income. A one-income family needs a larger contingency fund. The size of the emergency fund can also depend on your financial commitments. People with a paid-off house and no car payments might get by with a smaller cushion. This, by the way, is yet another reason to keep debt at a minimum.

Why have an emergency fund? We talked about the most serious scenario, having cash to live on if you lose your job. Other reasons include life's expected-but-unexpected cash drains. We don't know when they're coming but cash outlays for such expenses as car repairs, medical bills, and plumbing leaks are coming sooner or later. Without the cash to pay for these, you're likely to put them on a credit card and rack up finance charges. That just makes those "emergencies" more expensive.

Other reasons to have an emergency fund are less obvious. It can actually save you money. Think about it: With a cash cushion, you can feel comfortable saying no when a salesperson offers you an extended warranty. Why? Because you have the money to pay for the repairs if the item breaks. You can call your insurance agent and raise deductibles on your home and auto insurance, which will save you money on premiums.

Why? Because you have the cash to pay a higher deductible if you file a claim.

Maybe an emergency fund's greatest value is providing peace of mind, which any financially stressed-out person will tell you has a real dollar value.

Creating a rainy-day fund can be a two-step process. Although the long-term goal is a fund equal to three to six months' worth of bare-bones living expenses, a shorter-term goal might be to stash away $2,500. At that point, you haven't protected against job loss, but you have given yourself financial breathing room when the car and the clothes washer break down at the same time. Make the $2,500 emergency fund a high-priority goal. Fully funding the cash cushion can be balanced among your other financial priorities. For example, it would take a backseat to paying off high-interest debt.

That's especially true if you take a few steps to grow your emergency fund through noncash means. A cash horde is ideal, but in a crisis you simply need quick access to money, whether it's your own or someone else's.

Here are a few temporary moves to make in lieu of a fully funded emergency fund. These are in addition to your $2,500 in cash:

- **Establish a home-equity line of credit.** Homeowners could count home equity as part of their temporary emergency fund. A home-equity line is an open credit line against the equity you have built up in your house. It's cheap or free to open a line of credit, and you pay no interest unless you use it. If you use it, the interest you pay is likely to be tax deductible. With most HELOC accounts, you tap the line of credit by writing checks on the account or using a debit card to access the credit line. Apply for an equity line before a crisis occurs. Once disaster hits—you lose your job, for example—you might not qualify to open a HELOC. All that said, however, a home-equity line is not a good choice for compulsive spenders who will use the credit line for nonemergencies. And lenders have tightened requirements for getting a HELOC since the 2008 financial crisis. Improving your credit score will increase the chances of being approved for an equity line.

- **Raise your credit card limits.** Using high-interest credit cards is a very common but lousy way to address a financial emergency. If you're responsible with credit cards and rarely carry a balance, however, it couldn't hurt to ask your card company to raise your limits if you do it the right way. You must ask them to raise your maximum charge limit "without pulling my credit report." That way, the request will not damage your credit rating, as I said in Chapter 6, "Credit When Credit's Due." In fact, it could help your credit rating if you're successful because part of the credit score is based on the amount of used credit compared with the amount of available credit. A second advantage is the higher limit gives you a source of cash during a temporary cash-flow jam. There are more details about your credit cards in Chapter 6.

Once you're already in a money crisis with no emergency fund to tap, more desperate measures might be necessary. None of these options is an ideal solution:

- **Consider nonretirement investments.** Your regular investments outside of retirement plans might be mostly held in volatile stocks or in accounts that might charge an early withdrawal penalty, but these can be sources of emergency cash. True, using these funds in an emergency might force you to take an investment loss, but addressing a true crisis is usually more important.

- **Evaluate the bank of mom and dad.** Borrowing from relatives or friends is dicey at best, and should probably be among the last resorts in a crisis because it has ruined many relationships. But it could be a source of emergency money. One idea is to formalize such a loan by writing down the terms. Consider using loan documents from a place such as LawDepot.com or using a company such as CircleLending.com to formalize the paperwork.

- **Borrow or withdraw from a 401(k).** I hesitate to mention this option because unless you're desperate, it's a really bad idea. But you can borrow and withdraw from a 401(k) retirement account. There can be huge tax penalties and you'll lose growth on the money, which was supposed to go toward retirement. In the case of borrowing, you'll withdraw pretax money and pay yourself back with interest by using after-tax money. Then in retirement, you're taxed on withdrawals. So, you're being double-taxed on that money. Review with your plan administrator all the disadvantages of loans and withdrawals before going ahead. All that said, it *is* a source of cash if you're desperate. But consider this my attempt to nudge you away from this option.

In short, you need a rainy-day fund and a plan to access cash in a financial storm. It will, indeed, rain. It's just a matter of when.

2. Car Fund

Just like you will have financial emergencies, you *will* replace your vehicle. It's just a matter of when. Maybe no purchase gets consumers in more trouble than buying a car or truck. It's a two-headed problem.

First, people lust after cars they can't afford, which leads to five-year loans or longer and ridiculous leases (which is redundant because almost all leases are a ridiculous choice for people concerned with spending money smarter). People concentrate too much on the monthly payment, instead of how the purchase fits into their financial life. For the record, I'm obligated by all that's good and true in personal finance to urge you once again to buy a slightly used vehicle. That way, you avoid much of the new-car depreciation.

The second big mistake many people make is not putting down much money when buying a vehicle—or worse, rolling the payment of a previous vehicle into the loan on a new one. This leads to the brutal situation of actually owing more on a car than it's worth, or being "upside down." You can't sell the vehicle—or, if you get in a bad accident, you can't total the car—without losing thousands of dollars.

I don't want to get all ridiculous on you, but what if you paid cash for your next vehicle? In fact, I would argue that if you can't pay cash for a vehicle, you can't afford it.

Here's how to pay cash for your next vehicle: After you pay off your current vehicle, continue making the same monthly payment to yourself. Do that by making an automatic payment to a separate car-fund account. Then when you go to replace your vehicle, you'll have the trade-in value, plus cash saved in this account. That total becomes the purchase price of your new car, which you can now buy for cash. At the very least, you'll have a sizable down payment.

Here's just one example of how it would work: Keep your vehicle for four years after paying it off. If you were paying $400 a month, you would accumulate $19,200, plus interest, in your car fund. For simplicity, let's call it 20 grand. This, by the way, requires no additional sacrifice on your part. You've already been paying this $400 a month for several years.

If you get $5,000 by selling or trading in your old car, you can now pay $25,000 for a lightly used luxury car of your choosing.

How cool is that?

3. Seasonal Fund

This is an intentionally vague account. Customize it to fit short-term savings goals in your life. For example, you could use it for three major seasonal expenses, which happen to be spaced apart on the calendar. That means you can fund and deplete the account continually throughout the year. These seasonal expenses are as follows:

- **Holiday spending.** Gifts, travel, decorations, parties

- **Spring vacation.** Airfare, hotel, car rental
- **Back-to-school.** Clothing, school supplies, tuition, computers, textbooks

Another good idea is to have a separate account when you're saving for a house down payment. If you already own a house, you might create an account for home improvements, whether that's new siding, new furniture, or a kitchen remodel.

The running theme with any of these short-term savings accounts is to fund them regularly and automatically. That way, you'll have no trouble achieving those goals.

Retirement

Retirement investing for individuals is relatively new. A generation ago, most people had defined pensions, which meant that when you retired, you got a check every month. It was someone else's job to invest that money. Today, you're responsible, like it or not.

Retirement, 1-2-3

1. **Invest automatically.** Invest 10 percent of your income into a retirement plan, such as a 401(k) or Roth IRA.
2. **Diversify.** Invest all the money in a target-date retirement fund closest to when you'll retire.
3. **Hold on.** Never touch the money until you retire.

"Come on," you're thinking. "Entire books are written on retirement investing. How can it be this simple?"

It can. For the vast majority of people, this simple plan will work wonderfully. It's "good enough" to ensure you're saving for a respectable retirement. Of course, you can tweak this simple plan along the way, and probably should. But not doing these steps, or ones very similar, could mean you're in for a rough time in your golden years.

Just because it's simple, doesn't mean it's unsophisticated. And it certainly doesn't mean it's inferior. In fact, with investing, the more complicated things get, the more likely you'll be railroaded and some money manager is going to get rich off you.

Getting started with retirement saving is as easy as visiting your human resources department at work or going online to sign up for a retirement plan. If you started a new job, your employer might have enrolled you automatically. If you already have a retirement plan started, you can still use these steps by modifying your contributions and allocations.

How big of a retirement nest egg do you need to build? Whatever number you come up with is simultaneously supremely important and utterly meaningless.

You could assume you'll spend the same amount of money you do now, adjusted for inflation. But how reasonable is that, especially if you're in the wildly expensive raising-a-family stage of life?

Expenses in retirement often decrease. For example, you won't be funneling money into a retirement plan, child expenses are gone, and perhaps you paid off the home mortgage. On the other hand, you might need more money for traveling, recreation, and medical care.

Online calculators are a help in determining what you need because the math is complicated to do by hand. The more detailed—and unfortunately, tedious—the online questionnaire, the better your estimate will be. Examples of online calculators include the following:

- www.Fidelity.com/myPlan
- www3.troweprice.com/ric/RIC
- www.dinkytown.net
- www.choosetosave.org/ballpark
- www.aarp.org

Financial software, such as Quicken, also has retirement tools.

But realize that any dollar figure you come up with is just an educated guess. The best professional financial planners can only speculate about what the total dollar figure for your nest egg should be and what you need to be saving along the way to accumulate that dollar figure. That's because of the unknowable assumptions. These include everything from how long you'll live, to inflation rates, to what return your investments will earn. But an informed estimate is far better than none at all. It will give you a ballpark figure, so you know you're striving for either $750,000 in retirement savings or $4 million.

Focus on what you can control; that is, stashing away money automatically, keeping it diversified, and keeping your hands off it. The retirement goal might seem like an absurdly large number. But the only way to eat an elephant is one bite at a time.

1. Invest Automatically

As discussed previously, making retirement contributions automatic is fundamentally important. Employer retirement plans are great because the money disappears from your paycheck before you get it. The other good way is to fund a retirement account with automatic monthly transfers from your checking account.

Here are some basic questions and answers about investing for retirement:

- **Why should I save for retirement?** Because you'll reach an age where you don't want to work anymore, or physically (or mentally) can't. If you don't have savings earmarked for your retirement years, you'll be destitute or a burden to family members who will have to care for you.

- **Why make it automatic?** Retirement sounds like a long way off for many people. That makes it extremely difficult to make it a priority when the bustle of everyday life puts numerous demands on our money. With most people, if they have to write a check every month to their retirement plan, life will get in the way and they'll skip some months, or many months. But if you make it automatic, by contributing through a regular paycheck deduction or a regular draft from your checking account, you're more likely to succeed in saving regularly.

- **Why invest at least 10 percent?** Besides being a nice, round, easy-to-remember number, it's enough to start you on the path toward building retirement wealth. It also works well with the typical 401(k) plan, in which an employer matches the first 6 percent of whatever you contribute. You'll be guaranteed to capture all of that free money. And 10 percent is a good start toward 15 percent, a contribution goal many financial advisers suggest.

QUICK TIP

One painless way to get to 15 percent is to raise your contributions by 1 percent or 2 percent every time you get a pay raise. That way, you won't notice a reduction in your take-home pay.

- **Why use a retirement plan?** You could just squirrel away money in regular mutual funds for retirement. But when you use the umbrella of a retirement plan, you can shield the money from taxes, either now or later. If you pay less tax, you'll have more money in retirement.

- **Which retirement savings vehicle should I use?** This is where many people get bogged down. First, know that it's less important which retirement plan you choose. It's more important that you automatically contribute to a retirement plan—any retirement plan. That said, the following are brief descriptions of some of your choices:

  - **401(k) and 403(b).** If you qualify for a 401(k) retirement plan at work that matches your contributions, join the plan and contribute 10 percent of your income. This is the easiest solution. The 403(b) and 457 plans are similar. These plans have such complicated-looking names because they refer to part of the federal tax code. Considering it involves the IRS, what else would it be except complicated?

A 401(k) allows retirement money to grow tax free. The pain of contributing is reduced because less tax money will be deducted from your paycheck. So, contributing $100 to your 401(k) reduces your net pay by less than $100. The exact amount depends on your income-tax bracket and several other factors. With a 401(k), Uncle Sam gets his cut when you withdraw the money in retirement. It will be taxed at your regular income tax rate, whatever it is at that time.

QUICK TIP

If your employer matches your contributions, don't miss out on that free money! I've alluded to this previously, but it's worth emphasizing. Often an employer will contribute 3 percent of your pay if you contribute 6 percent. This is a fantastic deal. That's a 50 percent guaranteed return on your money. You can't get that anywhere else. Even if you dislike your employer plan, contribute at least enough to get the full matching contribution.

- **Roth IRA.** For those who don't have a 401(k) at work, open a Roth IRA and sign up to make regular contributions. With a Roth, you contribute money but get no up-front tax break. The benefit comes when you retire. That's when you can withdraw all the investment earnings contributed over the years, tax free. That's a huge advantage. The downsides are that higher-income people don't qualify to use a Roth and, if you do qualify, you can't stash away a ton of money—$5,000 a year in 2009 ($6,000 if you're age 50 or older). The earnings limits in 2009 were $120,000 if you're single and $176,000 if you're married. If your so-called "modified adjusted gross income," a line on your tax form, is larger than those limits, you can't use a Roth. And if your income is close to those limits, you might be allowed to make only a partial contribution of somewhat less than $5,000. Find updated limits and how to calculate modified adjusted gross income in IRS publication 590 at IRS.gov.

You can open a Roth IRA with many investment companies. Look for a place where you can make automatic contributions and one that has target-date retirement funds (more on that next, when we talk about diversifying your investments). You'll do well if you first check out Vanguard at www.vanguard.com, T. Rowe Price at www.troweprice.com, and Fidelity at www.fidelity.com.

Again, there are many ways to open a Roth IRA, including using a planner or broker and using a different family of mutual funds. But they probably will be more expensive because of broker commission and funds with high, built-in expenses.

- **What if I'm self-employed?** If you're self-employed, you probably have an accountant—or you should. Unless you'll make a hobby out of poring over income-tax strategies, taxes are often overly complicated for busy business owners. So, when it comes to investing for retirement, seek advice from your accountant. He or she will explain such retirement options as the individual 401(k), the SEP, and the SIMPLE IRA.

2. Diversify

So, once you have decided on a retirement account and resolved to invest automatically, which individual investments should you choose? You've probably heard, "Don't put all your eggs in one basket." You might have heard of "diversification." They both mean the same thing—spread your money around to different types of investments. Good diversification has been shown to reduce volatility and improve investment returns over time.

Again, this is where people get bogged down and confused. So, here's some simple advice that will be more than "good enough" for most people:

Put all your retirement money in a "target-date" fund closest to when you'll retire.

That's it, you're done.

"No way. It can't be that easy," you're thinking.

"Yes way. It can," I say.

Let's back up and talk about these "target-date" funds, sometimes called lifestyle funds. You've heard the phrase "the best thing since sliced bread?" Target-date retirement funds, at least the good ones, give sliced bread a run for its money. This is a one-stop-shop investment, a set-it-and-forget-it tool for retirement money, whether you're still working or already in retirement. Pick a year you'll probably retire, say 2030, and put all your retirement money into a 2030 target-date fund. Then you're on autopilot. Most employers nowadays offer these target-date options in 401(k) plans, and, of course, almost any mutual fund investment—including target-date funds—are an option in a self-directed retirement plan, such as an IRA or Roth IRA.

Everybody should know the basics of retirement planning, so following is the shortest primer on retirement allocations you'll ever see. But I contend that it suffices for most people.

- **Spread your money around.** Divvy up your money among major asset classes, typically U.S. stocks, foreign stocks, and bonds. Stocks, which refer to investing in private companies, are the higher-risk/higher-reward portion of your retirement bundle. Bonds are the safer portion. If one asset class grows quicker than the others, you have to "rebalance"—shift money around in your investments—to get them back in line with your targeted allocations.

- **Adjust your portfolio over time.** When you're younger, you can afford to take more risk because you have time to wait out any prolonged downturn in the market. Therefore, portfolios for younger people have a greater portion of stocks and less of bonds. Conversely, as you approach retirement or after you retire, you can't afford to take as much risk because you'll need the money soon. That's why you want more bonds and less stocks.

That brings us to target-date funds. Target funds do both of those things—diversify and rebalance—automatically.

How do you choose a good target-date fund? If you're in an employer-sponsored retirement plan, you probably only have one brand of target-date funds, so go with it. If you're choosing among all investments—in an IRA or Roth IRA, for example—choose one from one of these three companies:

- Vanguard, www.vanguard.com
- T. Rowe Price, www.troweprice.com
- Fidelity, www.fidelity.com

Of course, other companies offer good target-date funds too, but I'm here to make things easier. And these three companies offer excellent choices in target-date funds.

If you want a nudge in a specific direction for opening a new account, check out Vanguard. It has the lowest built-in expenses, which is a good thing and arguably, over the long haul, the most important thing. If you have the minimum $3,000 to open an account, put all of it, including future contributions, in the Vanguard Target Retirement fund with a year closest to when you'll retire. It will have a name like Vanguard Target Retirement 2030.

QUICK TIP: TWEAKING TARGET-DATE FUNDS

What if you want to take more risk than the average person with your retirement portfolio, or less risk? Simply choose a different target-date fund. If you want to take on more risk for the opportunity to get larger returns, choose a target-date fund with a date that's further away. It will have a higher portion in stocks. If you want less risk, choose a nearer target date. Don't know if you're a risk-taker? Take a quiz developed at Rutgers University, at http://njaes. rutgers.edu/money/riskquiz/. How freaked out did you get in 2008 when the stock market tanked? That's a very accurate measure of your risk tolerance.

What If Your Employer Doesn't Offer a Target-Date Fund?

If your 401(k) or other employer plan does not offer a target-date fund, retirement investing gets considerably more complicated. Get started by putting 60 percent in a broad stock index fund, such as a "total stock" index or "S&P 500" index. Put 20 percent in a foreign-stock index fund, and 20 percent in a bond index fund. But that's a generic and conservative allocation. You'll want to tweak that to fit your age and risk tolerance. One broad rule of thumb is to subtract your age from 120. That's the percentage of your retirement money that should be invested in stocks. The rest goes in bonds. So a 40-year-old would have 80 percent overall in stocks (60 percent U.S. stocks, 20 percent foreign) and

20 percent in bonds. If you're conservative, your stock-allocation percentage might be 100 minus your age.

You'll have to rebalance the allocations yourself, which again, refers to shifting money out of good-performing investments and putting the money into poorer performing ones. That's counterintuitive. But when you rebalance, you're essentially selling high and buying low, the most basic and best investing strategy. Rebalance at least once a year—on your birthday, for example—or when investment allocations get out of line by, say, 2 percent.

Why Index Funds?

An index mutual fund holds investments, such as stocks, that simply mimic an established index, such as the Standard & Poor's 500 Index. Index funds don't go searching for undervalued stocks ready to take off. In fact, index funds are dull and boring. And, oh yeah, they're superior to most funds you'll ever buy. Over time, index funds beat two-thirds to three-quarters of actively managed funds.

How can that be? It's because almost nobody, including the most brilliant minds on Wall Street, can consistently pick winning stocks over the long term. If some succeed over a short time, it's just as likely to be dumb luck as brilliance. Index funds are cheaper to operate because they don't have to pay for a big-salary stock picker. And they incur less tax costs because they trade less than actively managed funds. Therefore, more of the gains from the fund are passed along to you, the investor.

If you're going to invest in mutual funds, whether inside a retirement account or outside, choose index funds. In fact, the target-date retirement funds I'm so fond of are the Vanguard ones. Why? You guessed it: It's a bundle of index funds.

This notion about index funds being superior to stock-picking funds is a fascinating topic. A famous book that lays out why it's true is *A Random Walk Down Wall Street* by Burton G. Malkiel.

QUICK TIP

The amount of retirement contributions to put in your company stock should be zero percent, nada, nothing. You rely on this company for your income. That's plenty of your financial life tied to a single company. If you want to invest some "gambling" money in company stock, go for it. Another exception might be if a generous company match is doled out in company stock. But do not invest retirement money that you're counting on in company stock.

Already have retirement money in company stock? Sell it—gradually, if you prefer—and invest the money in a target-date fund or well-diversified portfolio of funds. Hope I wasn't unclear on this point.

3. Hold On

Study after study shows that retirement investors are lousy at timing the financial markets, especially the stock market. They get out of the market when it's low and everybody is scared and discouraged. Then, they get in when the market is high and everybody is euphoric and optimistic.

Of course, their returns are far worse than they would have been if those investors just stayed the course. Keeping your money out of the market and missing just a few days of the best run-ups can have long-lasting effects—meaning you'll retire with significantly less money than if you had just held on.

Richard Thaler, the professor of behavioral science and economics at the University of Chicago whom I mentioned in the introduction, had this to say during one depressed period in the stock market:

"I have not looked at any of my holdings and don't intend to. I don't want to be tempted to jump because I think I'd be more likely to jump in the wrong direction than the right one. My advice has always been to choose a sensible diversified portfolio and stop reading the financial pages. I recommend the sports section."

401(k) Rollovers

It's a good idea to transfer money from the retirement plan of an old employer—or several old employers—into an IRA, where you have more investment choices, including target-date retirement funds. That involves some paperwork with your previous employer's human resources department and the fund company you'll use for your IRA. Again, Vanguard, T. Rowe Price, and Fidelity are good choices for IRAs because they are low-cost. It's important to use a direct transfer for the rollover money. The HR department will know how to do this. If the old employer sends you a check, you risk suffering a huge tax hit because the IRS will assume you withdrew all the money for nonretirement use.

Saving for College

The most important thing to know about saving for kids' college expenses is to realize it's not your top financial priority. You're not a bad parent if you don't save 100 percent of the money needed to send your child to an Ivy League college. Eliminating high-interest debt, creating an emergency fund, and regularly contributing 10 percent or more of your income to a retirement plan come first.

Why retirement savings first? Because you can get grants and low-interest loans for college. No bank is going to lend you money for retirement. And how much are your kids going to appreciate having their college paid for if at age 75 you have to move in with them because you didn't save enough for retirement?

Saving for College, 1-2-3

1. **Open a 529 college savings account online.**
2. **Select an age-based plan.**
3. **Contribute automatically.**

If you look at projections for college costs, you might start feeling ill. You can find costs and use calculators at the College Board Web site, found at www.collegeboard.com. Others are at Savingforcollege.com, Dinkytown.com, and FinAid.org.

For a newborn, you'd have to save about $180,000 to pay the cost of sending the child to a state university. A private university? About $367,000. But those are the scare-you-to-death numbers that stray from reality.

Relatively few students pay the full "sticker price" for going to college. Besides growing college savings over the years, you'll potentially have scholarships, loans, grants, and other forms of financial aid. In fact, the average yearly cost of a four-year public school in 2008–09 was just $6,585, according to the College Board. Over four years, that's about $26,000, or about the cost of a modest new car.

Another problem with those scary numbers? It's probably not even wise to save 100 percent of college costs. What if your child doesn't end up going to college? What if through new government programs the costs for college decline? What if your savings grow faster than expected and you have too much saved?

All that said, college is expensive and the sooner you can start saving, the better.

The biggest problem with saving for college is it can be complicated. There seem to be a million and one details, some of which don't seem to make much sense. That's why I'm going to simplify it for you and give you one, single suggestion.

Go to www.uesp.org and open a 529 college savings plan, called the Utah Educational Savings Plan. You don't have to be a resident of Utah to participate and your child does not have to go to school in Utah. It's just a cookie jar to stash the money so you get a huge federal tax break when you withdraw the money.

In the Utah plan, choose age-based plan No. 8, called Diversified-B. Contribute at least $50 per month, raising regular contributions when you can. You can always transfer to a different plan later if you have a good reason. It's more important to get started than to pick the absolute best college savings plan. In fact, there are good reasons for choosing other plans. But choice No. 8 in the Utah college savings plan is "good enough" for almost anyone. Just get it started.

Here are the details on college savings.

1. Open a 529 College Savings Account Online

You have many ways to save money for college, but only one is a clear choice for almost everybody. Just like 401(k) and 403(b) retirement plans, the best college savings vehicle has a weird name, derived from the federal tax code that allows it. It's called a Section 529 college savings account.

The basic deal with a Section 529 account is you put money into investments within the account over the years, in lump sums, monthly installments, or both. The money is usually invested in a mix of investments, such as stocks, mutual funds, and bonds. That way, the money is likely to grow so you can pay more and borrow less when it's time to pay—or help pay—for college. Of course, you could do that in regular mutual funds. The big benefit of investing within a 529 account comes when you take money out to pay for college costs at any accredited school. Growth on that money through the years—the gain—is free of federal tax. That's a huge advantage, likely to amount to literally thousands of dollars that go to paying for your kid's tuition, rather than funding Uncle Sam's kitty.

Another advantage of 529 plans is you can contribute a lot of money. It varies by state, but caps are typically around $300,000. And anybody can contribute, including grandparents and other relatives. The money can be used not only for college tuition, but also for room and board, and books and supplies, including a computer.

If your kid doesn't go to college—or, heaven forbid, dies—you can transfer the account to another relative or use it yourself. The definition of a family relative is generous, extending to such familial relationships as step-children, nieces, nephews, and first cousins. If you don't use the money for college, you'll have to pay a 10 percent penalty on withdrawals plus income taxes. One exception is if your kid gets a scholarship, you can withdraw money equal to the scholarship amount without paying the 10 percent penalty. But you will have to pay income taxes on the money's growth.

Opening an Account

How do you start a 529 account? That's both easy and hard. But mostly, it's worth it, to keep Uncle Sam's hands off money earmarked for college.

It's easy because once you choose a 529 plan, you just fill out forms and mail a check (or fund it by electronic transfer from a bank account). Some plans let you do all that online. That's it. You've successfully opened a 529 college savings plan. Make sure to open separate accounts for each child, but register accounts in parents' names. That's so you, as a parent, control the investments, and the student might end up qualifying for more financial aid.

Because opening a 529 account is so easy, there's no reason to go through a stockbroker, insurance salesperson, or financial planner. More important, opening an account by yourself is free. A financial professional is likely to put you in a plan that includes commissions and management fees that will retard growth on your college-savings money. That means you'll probably have a smaller total when it comes time to pay college bills.

Professionals don't have access to better plans than you do as an individual.

Choosing a Plan

Where people get bogged down is trying to choose among all the different plans. Section 529 plans are operated through state governments. So, most states offer their own 529 plans. Here's the confusing part: You can pick from most any state's savings plan, and your child can go to school in any state. That means you're not locked into your own state's plan.

That sounds like good news. But there are so many plans with so many different features, costs, and investment choices, it's almost impossible to compare them all in any intelligent way.

But take heart. You can transfer your 529 plan once a year. So, you're not locked into your first choice. You can always change it later.

That's why, to make things simple, I recommend just one: the Utah Educational Savings Plan, found at www.uesp.org. The Utah plan is on virtually every respected list of top-tier 529 plans. It has low fees and great investment choices.

Is the Utah plan the absolute best choice for everybody? Not necessarily. But it's a darned good choice, and it's "good enough" to get you started so you can get on with your life. Opening and regularly contributing to a decent college savings plan is far more important than which one you choose.

Should You Transfer Your 529 Account?

Already have a 529 plan started? It might not be worth switching. When 529 plans first started, some were real stinkers. Fortunately for parents, many states have improved their plans by cutting fees and offering better investment options.

"529 college-savings plans continue to get better," says respected mutual fund analysis firm Morningstar, which each year reports on the best and worst 529 plans. "Several years ago, many were high-cost messes. Since then, some [lousy choices] have been spruced up and others have been shut down. The important thing is that more people using these vehicles to save for college are getting a good deal." Go to www.Savingforcollege. com, and see how your plan is rated. If it receives a rating of four graduation "caps" or more out of a possible five, you're fine where you are. For example, I started years ago with the 529 plan in Iowa. It's not always at the very top of ratings I see, but it's usually in the top few. The Iowa plan received a four-cap rating from www.Savingforcollege.com. As a general rule of thumb, if the plan manager has the name Vanguard or Upromise/Vanguard, T. Rowe Price, Fidelity, and to a lesser extent TIAA-CREF, it's probably a decent plan.

If you're in a plan with high expenses and live in a state with no tax breaks for 529 plans, you should accelerate your search for a new plan. Your new plan will give you instructions on how to transfer money from the old plan to the new one. If you want to shop around for a more optimal 529 plan—and don't want to take my advice to use the Utah plan—here are the primary considerations:

- **Fund expenses.** The most important fees are those charged by the mutual fund companies and those charged by states to administer the college savings plan. These fees might seem insignificant, 1 percent or lower each, but they add up to a lot of lost money over time. States might also charge flat fees for opening and maintaining an account. Compare costs and other features at www.saving-forcollege.com/compare_529_plans/.

- **Allocations.** Though most 529 plans offer age-based investment options, they spread the money around differently among types of investments. Look for a broad allocation among U.S. and foreign stocks, as well as bonds. And always prefer index funds, rather than actively managed funds.

- **State tax breaks.** Some states won't tax your gains in a 529 plan, although many require you to use your own state's plan to get that break. Others allow you to take a tax deduction on your income tax form for money you contributed. These goodies from state governments are nice and could be considered as you choose a plan. But they probably won't make up for high expenses and lousy fund choices.

Here, briefly are non-529 options for college savings that I skipped earlier.

- **Prepaid tuition plans.** With these, also called guaranteed plans, you essentially buy college credits at today's prices. They're good for the same number of credits when your kid goes to school. So, the return on your investment is about equal to the price inflation in college tuition costs. This might be a good choice if you just want to preserve the value of money against tuition increases and you don't care about growing it to pay for more semesters. Or, if you can't stand to see the value of your college nest egg ebb and flow with stock and bond markets, the guaranteed program might be best. Some states require residency to use these plans. And many states only allow you to pay for tuition and fees with prepaid money, not room and board.

Starting in 2004, individual educational institutions were allowed to offer their own prepaid tuition plans. The Independent 529 Plan is such an offering by a group of private colleges. More information can be found at www.independent529plan.org, or 1-888-718-7878.

To add to confusion, all these prepaid plans are technically 529 plans too. However, most people call these "prepaid tuition plans" and the investment-style plans "529 plans." One strategy might be to use both an investment-style 529 and a prepaid 529.

- **Coverdell Education Savings Account.** There's nothing terribly wrong with these accounts, formerly called ESAs. The main drawback is you can only contribute $2,000 a year per child. Otherwise, they're similar to a 529 plan. The big advantage as of this writing is you can use them to pay for private school expenses before college. However, unless Congress acts before 2010, contribution limits revert to the old cap of $500 per year, and you can't use the money for elementary or secondary private school.

• **Custodial accounts.** These accounts are called Uniform Gift to Minors Act (UGMA) and Uniform Transfer to Minors Act (UTMA). They were the primary way to save for college before creation of 529 plans in 1996. However, they have lost almost all of their appeal as college-savings vehicles, when compared with 529 plans. If you already have an UGMA or UTMA, feel free to liquidate the account and put the money in a 529 college savings plan or prepaid plan, or convert to a 529 plan with the help of your accountant and the 529 plan administrator.

2. Select an Age-Based Plan

Most 529 plans include an option to invest all of your college savings in a single diversified mutual fund. It's an age-based fund invested aggressively when children are young and more conservatively when children approach college age. Unless you have a specific investing philosophy or don't need the money to grow much, these age-based funds are the way to go.

Age-based funds automatically reallocate money to more conservative investments as your child nears college enrollment. When your children are toddlers, the money would mostly be invested in stocks. When they reach high school, the money shifts to more conservative holdings.

For example, in the recommended Utah No. 8 plan, Diversified-B, a toddler would have money invested this way: 56 percent U.S. stocks, 24 percent foreign stocks, and 20 percent bonds. As the child ages, money shifts from stocks to bonds. The other age-based options in the Utah plan are fine too. I like Diversified-B, mostly because it includes a decent portion of foreign stocks. It also provides finer diversification among stocks from companies of all sizes.

Does this automatic investing sound familiar? These are similar to target-date retirement funds, only college is the target date, rather than retirement. They are the no-brainer, set-it-and-forget-it option that is more than "good enough."

QUICK TIP

If you have a huge lump sum to deposit into an account, rather than trying to grow monthly contributions, you should probably choose a more conservative allocation.

Just like you can switch 529 plans once every 12 months, you can also switch investment strategies within a 529 plan once within a year's time. So, you're only stuck with your allocation for one year, if you decide you don't like it.

3. Contribute Automatically

We've talked about the importance of making savings automatic. It's the same for college savings. Contribute with regular deposits in your 529 account by setting up automatic monthly withdrawals from your checking account.

Formulate a plan to raise the contributions annually, when you get a raise or at a predetermined time, such as the child's birthday. And consider funding the account with portions of such windfalls as a federal tax refund, annual salary bonus, or cash gift. As you finish paying off debt, you can funnel more money into college savings. For example, if paying off an automobile is your last nonmortgage debt, redirect at least part of that payment to college savings. Again, that's assuming your other priorities, such as paying off high-interest debt, funding retirement, and building an emergency fund, are all under way.

Quick Tip

Boosts to your college savings plans can come via rewards programs, where your everyday spending via credit cards or online shopping portals contributes small amounts to college savings. Find details at Upromise.com, BabyMint.com, and Littlegrad.com.

Community College Route

Saving for four-year college expenses is a swell idea. But if you really want to chop down the price tag, consider sending your child to a community college for the first two years. They would then transfer to a name-brand university to get a four-year degree diploma. It's what I call the two-year, two-year plan.

The cost of tuition and fees at community colleges is typically half of public four-year schools and about one-tenth the cost of private colleges. Studies show students taking the community college route are just as prepared as those who go to four-year schools, and earn just as much money after they graduate.

They might even get a better education in those introductory classes. Courses at community colleges are taught by teachers who often have real-world experience working in their fields. Introductory classes at four-year schools are often taught by teaching assistants or professors more interested in research than education.

Choosing a Financial Adviser

Americans today are forced to make a dizzying array of financial decisions, including many we've talked about in this book: how to build a retirement nest egg, save for kids' college expenses, and deal with debt and insurance.

For help, you might consider hiring a personal financial adviser. That can be a great idea or a bad one. The main advice: Buyer beware.

Choosing a Financial Adviser, 1-2-3

1. Interview three fee-only planners.
2. Ask questions and listen to your gut.
3. Never agree to an investment you don't understand.

The title "financial adviser" is not regulated. No government body dictates who can call themselves one. So, anybody can print up business cards and call himself or herself a financial adviser. It's up to you to weed out bad advisers from good. To do that, you'll need to know the insider secrets of the financial planning industry.

The first thing to know is that you shouldn't abdicate responsibility and turn over your financial life to someone else, no matter how good the adviser is. Hiring a financial adviser is not like hiring a lawn service to cut your grass. In that case, you're hiring the lawn service to perform a specific task so you don't have to. A financial adviser should be different. It's like asking a landscaper for advice on how best to cut your grass. He might pull-start the mower for you and walk alongside. But ultimately, you'll guide the mower and navigate around the yard. And you'll have to live with the result.

So, hiring an adviser should be a partnership or coaching relationship, rather than work-for-hire. A good adviser will help identify problems, set goals, suggest strategies, and provide objective opinions.

1. Interview Three Fee-Only Planners

The biggest problem with most financial advisers is they have divided loyalties. On one hand, they might truly want to help you achieve your goals and get you the best returns on investments. However, that can be in direct conflict with other goals, which are to keep their job, feed their own family, and provide themselves a good income. That brings us to this unfortunate fact:

Financial advisers make more money if they put you in bad investments.

Why? Because many get commissions—call them kickbacks, if you like—from the investment companies where they put your money. Sometimes, the worst investments offer the biggest kickbacks. Advisers at insurers and brokerages might be good and decent people, but their first and foremost job is to sell you financial products.

A similar conflict would be going to a doctor who doesn't charge for office visits but is paid by drug companies for selling you pills. Any chance his prescription pad would be a little busier, whether you really needed drugs or not?

The solution? Use a fee-only planner.

A fee-only planner is paid only by you, not financial companies. Beware that the term "fee-based" is entirely different. That means the adviser is compensated by both fees and commissions. Fee-only advisers often charge by the hour or by a percentage of your assets that the adviser manages. Ideally, you would pay for advice and implement the recommendations yourself. But if the adviser will manage your money, a management fee amounting to 1 percent of your assets is reasonable, while 2.5 percent is too much. Either way, be sure the planner is using the right tools—our good friends, no-load index funds.

Two good online sources for finding fee-only planners are NAPFA.org and GarrettPlanningNetwork.com. Each of these Web sites has a "find-a-planner" option to help you locate an adviser near you.

This is important: All that said, there are many good commission-based financial advisers that would do a fantastic job for you. I just think the built-in conflict of interest is too important to overlook. Conversely, just because an adviser is fee-only doesn't mean he or she is any good.

Once you have a short list of fee-only advisers, schedule an in-person interview, which should be free of charge. That might seem time consuming, but it's worthwhile. Come prepared with your financial information, such as how much income you have and all your investment balances.

As you set out to choose an adviser, think about what specific help you need. Do you feel helpless in choosing mutual funds? Don't know what to do with stock options you received at work? Are you worried you don't have the right insurances or financial documents, such as a will, living will, and medical power of attorney? Do you need advice on spending an inheritance? Do you want a comprehensive plan to cover all aspects of your money life?

Before setting up the interview, make sure the planner hasn't been in trouble. Find out about disciplinary actions by going to the U.S. Securities and Exchange Commission Web site at www.sec.gov or calling 1-800-SEC-0330. Look for a link like "Check Out Brokers & Advisers." You can also contact your state agency that oversees investment advisers. For advisers who sell investments, otherwise known as stockbrokers, you can conduct a BrokerCheck at the FINRA Web site, brokercheck.finra.org, or call 1-800-289-9999.

2. Ask Questions and Listen to Your Gut

Choosing the right adviser breaks down into three basic tasks: Assessing the adviser's technical competence, trustworthiness, and compatibility with you. Here are six questions that will help you judge an adviser, whether they are fee-only or not:

- **How are you paid?** This might be an uncomfortable question to ask. But it is fundamental and important. If you're using a fee-only planner, the answers should be straightforward. Ask the planner for his or her Form ADV, a document that describes the fee structure.

- **What are your qualifications?** Choose a planner who has been in the business for several years and has a certification, such as Certified Financial Planner or CFP. (See sidebar for other certifications.) Ask about work history.

ABCs of Financial Certifications

The financial services industry has an alphabet soup of acronyms that represent certifications for financial advisers. Unfortunately, none assures you of a competent or ethical adviser. Designations are awarded by private organizations that don't answer to government regulators. However, an official designation after an adviser's name at least signals he or she probably passed a test of basic financial concepts and is staying current on changes. The following are a few of the more meaningful certifications:

- **CFP: Certified Financial Planner.** Among the most popular of financial planning certifications, CFPs must have at least five years of planning experience or a bachelor's degree plus three years of financial planning experience. They must also complete a five-course program, pass a 10-hour comprehensive exam, complete 30 hours of continuing education every two years, and adhere to ethics standards.

- **ChFC: Chartered Financial Consultant.** ChFCs must complete three more courses than the CFPs but only have to pass individual topic exams, not a comprehensive exam. They must have three years of experience in the financial services industry and adhere to ethical standards. They must also complete 30 hours of continuing education every two years.

- **CFA: Chartered Financial Analyst.** A designation geared more toward the specialty of investing and portfolio management than broader areas of personal finance. CFAs must pass three rigorous exams covering economics, financial accounting, portfolio management, securities analysis, and ethics, and have approved work experience.

- **CPA-PFS: Certified Public Accountant-Personal Financial Specialist.** The PFS designation is awarded to CPAs who have a minimum of 1,400 hours of financial planning business experience, completed continuing education within the last five years, passed an exam, and adhere to a code of ethics.

  For brief information on other designations, go online to Finra.org and click "Investor Information," then "Professional Designations."

- **What is your financial planning philosophy?** Here, you're fishing for a comfort level. The adviser should talk about his or her planning process and not about hot stocks or unusual investments. If a prospective financial adviser says he or she can beat the market and promises big investment returns, end the meeting. Nobody can predict market movements. The adviser is either a fool or a liar, and probably a cheat. A good financial adviser will make sure you're well-diversified, so you can limit risk and maximize returns.

  As the adviser explains his or her philosophy, ask yourself: Are you being coached or sold to? And get a feel for how rushed the adviser is. If he or she doesn't have time to attract you as a client, the adviser might not have time for you after you become one. Finally, note the words and tone the adviser uses. Is he or she speaking in financial jargon, knowing you won't understand? It actually takes greater skill and knowledge to explain things simply. Is the tone condescending or supportive?

- **What services do you offer?** If you need a broad spectrum of advice, make sure the planner can help with insurance, tax planning, investments, estate planning, and retirement planning. This is the time to ask whether the adviser will be the only person you deal with, or whether you'll be shuffled off to a junior associate. And ask about how the adviser will communicate, by e-mail or phone, for example. Will you receive regular reports and periodic reviews about your financial status?

- **Tell me about your typical client.** You want an adviser accustomed to working with people like you. If the adviser typically works with multimillionaires and you have total assets of $100,000, how much attention do you think you'll get? You should also ask for a sample financial plan for a client in similar circumstances to yours—with the client's name removed, of course.

- **Can I contact referrals?** Granted, an adviser is only going to refer you to his happy clients. Ask the client, "If you had to do it again, would you pick this planner?" and "What is the downside of working with this planner?"

You want to gather factual information, but trust your gut, too. That doesn't mean you should judge whether you like the adviser as a person or whether you hit it off in idle chitchat. That's irrelevant. This is a business relationship, not a personal one.

Although some people are more gullible than others, your gut should guide you, especially if you go into the meeting with a bit of skepticism. It will tell you if the adviser is being evasive or is snowing you.

3. Never Agree to an Investment You Don't Understand

If you can't explain it to your teenager or your elderly mother, don't do it.

This is a great rule because it can keep you out of harm's way. For example, there are few average Americans who can thoroughly and accurately explain what a variable annuity is. They're wildly complicated. And that works out fine. They're not good investments for most people anyway.

That's not to say you shouldn't endeavor to learn more about finance basics. You shouldn't shy away from stock mutual funds because you're not quite certain what they are.

There are many good resources for investing basics, including books and Web sites. One free resource is at the *Los Angeles Times* newspaper Web site. It has a "Money Library" with a host of finance topics, including investing. It's at www.latimes.com.

All this due diligence in hiring a financial planner might seem daunting, but don't let it deter you from getting the help you need. Starting on the right financial track, even using a mediocre but ethical planner, is better than doing nothing. And remember, you can always switch financial advisers later.

Endnotes

1. On October 3, 2008, Congress temporarily increased FDIC deposit insurance from $100,000 to $250,000 per depositor through December 31, 2009. As of this writing, it is uncertain whether the raised limit will become permanent. Learn more at www.fdic.gov.

Chapter 8

Putting It All Together

Succeeding with Money

In the introduction of this book, I promised to help you navigate the world of spending and saving money. I said this book would be like a GPS device that helps you with driving directions. I wanted to get you from here to there safely and with the fewest hassles.

I've touched on the vast majority of money issues that you will probably encounter in your life. Did I cover every detail of every money topic? No. Few books do. And I didn't even try.

What I wanted to do is to make money simple. I did that by breaking down common money topics to their three most-important tasks. I gave you very specific advice. And granted, it might not be the absolute best advice you could possibly receive. But it's darned fine advice for almost everybody. It nudges you toward money decisions that are "good enough." That allows you to make money decisions and get on with your life. You can take comfort in the fact that you're doing smart things with your hard-earned cash.

We even had some fun along the way. What other personal finance book tells you how to make razor blades last longer, how to get the best deals on video cables, and how to spend $20 a year on phone service?

I hope you'll go through the topics in this book and methodically address each area of your money life—after all, each contains just three steps.

Throughout this book, I used a 1-2-3 format, which defined tasks for each money topic. But what if I were to give you just one more 1-2-3 list? This would be a super–Cliff Notes version. It would be three steps to succeeding with money.

If you did nothing else in this whole book, doing these three things will give you a shot at being a financial winner.

Based on my knowledge of money topics and based on feedback from literally thousands of readers over the years, that list would look like the following:

Succeeding with Money, 1-2-3

1. **Never buy a new car until you're a millionaire.**
2. **Buy a home that you can afford.**
3. **Care about spending.**

I briefly mentioned cars and houses in other chapters. They are the largest single purchases most people

will make in their lifetimes. Financing for these two purchases often ranks at the top of most people's monthly
expenditures. For that reason, they are important.

But you already know that. You probably already
take great pains to be a smart consumer about vehicles
and houses. Whether you succeed is a different matter.

What you might not have contemplated is the vast
difference between buying a car and buying a house.
They impact your money life in dramatically different
ways. They are different for two fundamental reasons.
The reasons are:

- The value of your vehicle is guaranteed to plum-
  met. (That's bad.)
- The value of your house almost always rises.
  (That's good.)

These might seem like terribly elementary observa-
tions. But from a bird's-eye view overlooking the span
of your money life, there is profound wisdom in recog-
nizing these truths. Is the money you're spending working for you or against you?

1. Never Buy a New Car Until You're a Millionaire

Get-out-of-debt guru Dave Ramsey often says this. He
has a flair for dramatic statements, and I agree with this
one, so I stole it.

If a new car costs $30,000 and it loses the standard
30 percent of its value in its first year, that depreciation
costs $9,000.

Is $9,000 a lot of money in your world? If so, you should always buy one-year-old or older cars. In other words, don't buy a new car until you're a millionaire. It doesn't get much more complicated than that.

But car-buying isn't that easy, is it? Confusion sets in when you start talking about your dream car or how low the monthly payments are or how unreliable a used car might be. Somehow new-car smell warps our brains and clouds the issue.

Vehicles today are more reliable than ever. Even a three-year-old car is still a pup. Some of the reliable family sedans with minimal maintenance go 150,000 miles without a hiccup. See Chapter 7, "How to Save Money," for details on setting up a car fund to save enough to pay cash for your next vehicle.

QUICK TIP:

Need to ease into the buying-used-cars thing? Try a certified preowned car with a warranty from the manufacturer, not the dealer or a third party. Certified cars are more expensive than noncertified, but this might give you the peace of mind you need to move from buying new to buying used. By the way, isn't "preowned" a silly way to describe a used car? Preowned literally means "before it's owned," or new.

---

2. Buy a Home That You Can Afford

Let's split this task into two parts. The first half, "buy a home" is a recommendation to buy a house instead of renting.

The value of a home comes partly from its price appreciation. Generally, house prices increase over the long term. The house-price bubble that started bursting in 2006 was an exception.

Homeowners also get another kind of value, however. They don't have to pay rent. Instead, they pay on a mortgage, which ends up being a form of forced savings. When renters pay rent, they never see that money again. Meanwhile, homeowners are building equity in the property, assuming they don't have one of those exotic "negative amortization" loans that were all the rage just before the housing bubble.

And if homeowners itemize their tax deductions, they can claim their mortgage interest, which is yet another financial benefit.

A home mortgage also provides leverage. You put down a small fraction of the home's worth in the form of a down payment. But when you sell the home, you get to keep the gain on the entire home's value—not just the down payment portion. For example, imagine you bought a home for $300,000 with a 20 percent down payment of $60,000. If you sell the house for $500,000, you get to keep all the $200,000 gain, not just 20 percent of it.

And you lock in your housing costs. Rents might rise every year, but assuming you got a 30-year fixed-rate mortgage, your payment will be the same for decades.

Consider this startling statistic: The average homeowner has a net worth of nearly $200,000, while the average renter has a net worth of less than $5,000, according to the Federal Reserve Survey of Consumer

Finances. And it's not because homeowners have 40 times the income of renters; they only have about twice as much.

The second half of this "buy a home" task is the qualifier "that you can afford." This is where so many people messed up during the housing crisis. Because of weirdo mortgages that artificially lowered the monthly payment, many people bought homes they could not afford in the long run.

One rule of affordability comes from the Federal Housing Administration. It contends that your monthly payment for mortgage principal and interest, plus real estate taxes, plus homeowner's insurance should not exceed 29 percent of your gross income. So, if your household income is $8,000 a month, you could afford a total monthly payment of $2,320.

That's fairly liberal. I might even classify that as a "stretch" payment, meaning you'll probably feel pinched until your income rises over the years. Remember, the principal-and-interest part of your house payment stays the same with a fixed-rate mortgage. So, when your income rises, the payment becomes easier to make.

If you were going to stretch to afford a house payment or a car payment, the house is the one to choose.

You can play with mortgage-affordability calculators on the Internet at such Web sites as Bankrate.com and Dinkytown.com to hone in on a comfortable payment for you.

3. Care about Spending

And this is what it's all about. Remember that spending and saving aren't really different. Saving is just an intellectual decision to spend later, rather than now. If most people put as much time and effort into managing their money lives as managing their weekly TV watching, they would be far better off.

And daily spending matters. From supermarket shopping to your phone bills to insurance. You'll be far wealthier if you can develop the spending smart philosophy: Spend on purpose, rather than by accident and habit. And plug the leaks of wasteful spending, so you can funnel more money to things you truly care about.

Earning is important, but you can't outearn dumb spending.

So, care about all your spending, whether you're spending today, yesterday, or tomorrow. It's as easy as 1-2-3.

For more information about saving and spending smart, see my blog at SpendingSmart.net and my Web site at www.GregKarp.com. Feel free to e-mail me at greg@gregkarp.com.

Index